EDUCATING TO EMPOWER!

HANDBOOK
for
EVANGELISTS & MINISTERS

A Comprehensive Guide & Teaching Manual for Ministers of the Gospel

DR. GLORIES POWELL

HANDBOOK for Evangelists & Ministers
A Comprehensive Guide & Teaching Manual for Ministers of the Gospel

Printed in the USA. First Printing 2017.

Published by Kingdom House Publishing | Lakebay, WA | www.kingdomhouse.net

KINGDOM HOUSE
P U B L I S H I N G

ISBN (print): 978-1-939944-37-5

ISBN (electronic): 978-1-939944-38-2

Library of Congress Control Number (LCCN): 2017908661

Unless otherwise noted, Scripture quotations have been taken from the King James Version of the Bible. The King James Version of the Bible is a work in the public domain.

To contact the author:
Dr. Glories Powell
GLORIES POWELL MINISTRIES
P.O. Box 335224
North Las Vegas, NV 89033
Email: gpministries@cox.net

WWW.DRGPOWELL.COM

DEDICATION

THIS HANDBOOK IS DEDICATED TO
EVERY MINISTER OF THE GOSPEL WHO
KNOWS THEY MUST MODEL THEIR
MESSAGE AND LIVE WHAT THEY TEACH.
IT WAS WRITTEN FOR ALL THOSE
SEEKING TO BECOME SKILLED IN
PRESENTING THE WORD OF GOD.

WHAT OTHERS SAY ABOUT
HANDBOOK FOR EVANGELISTS & MINISTERS

This is a very "Theo-logical" approach to the issue of disorganized and dislocated approaches to administering truth in the church today. God is not "logical" in the sense of bowing to the tenets of fleshly ideas and intellect, but He is logical in the sense of having a purpose, a process and a presentation in how things are properly done. He is "logical" indeed. It is from the term *logos* that we arrive at the word "logic." Pure spiritual logic is indeed based on the *Logos* Word of God. The material in this book by Dr. Powell restores that much needed orderly approach to carrying out the missions and mandates of the church from a biblical perspective rather than throwing caution to the wind disguised as "flowing in the Spirit." This manual is well proportioned and packaged to give today's ministers the much needed tools to progressively lead God's people. Great job Dr. Powell!

DR. GORDON E. BRADSHAW
President—Global Effect Movers & Shakers (GEMS) Network
Author: *The Technology of Apostolic Succession, Authority for Assignment,* and *I SEE THRONES!*
www.gemsnetwork.org

Dr. Glories Powell is a prolific teacher, and a didactic preacher. The *Handbook for Evangelists & Ministers* will stimulate the readers' creative ability to rightly divide the Word of Truth. Ministry instructors, mentors, and developers, will treasure this book because of its unique and comprehensive approach to teaching doctrine. It is a must-read for anyone seeking to further their biblical education and should be a part of the library of any ministry.

BISHOP JEFFERY D. GOLDSMITH BA, MA, D.D.
Senior Pastor—Emmanuel Tabernacle
Vice President—Aenon Bible College
Diocesan Bishop—Oklahoma District Council, Inc.
Pentecostal Assemblies of the World, Inc.
www.emmanueltabernacleok.com

Handbooks such as this one are essential tools and excellent foundations in any field to provide the theoretical and practical truths, standards, norms, protocols, techniques and building blocks for professional practice and competency. Dr. Powell is an experienced and educated minister and has provided a clear, concise, and compelling training manual for ministers and evangelists. I highly recommend it and heartily endorse it. Buy it. Read it. Apply it.

DR. BRUCE COOK
Chair—Kingdom Congressional International Alliance (KCIA)
Author of *Partnering with the Prophetic* and *Aligning with the Apostolic*
www.kcialliance.org

CALLED ORDAINED DEDICATED ANOINTED

When I became Pastor of CODA Ministries and CEO of The Moment of Truth Ministries, Inc., I developed an operations manual which also contained a small section of instructions for ministers. It's been ten years since I wrote the CODA operations manual. Since then, there has been a tremendous moral and spiritual decline in our churches across the nation, and the need for a comprehensive, ministry teaching manual has increased. Pastors, evangelists, and ministers are facing the challenging task of teaching and preaching the message of the Kingdom, many times without formal seminary education, to an over-educated, often condescending and resistant audience.

The **Handbook for Evangelists and Ministers**, written as a reference guide and training manual for those called to ministry, will provide valuable tools that will help in fulfilling their Divine assignment. We believe the function of the Church is to produce Kingdom citizens. We, as skilled Ministers, have a Biblical mandate to build and train people in that process. As the caterpillar goes through a threefold process of change, being confined in the cocoon before it emerges as a beautiful butterfly, the Believer also experiences a time of metamorphosis. The caterpillar represents the unsaved and the new convert; the cocoon represents times of trials and challenges, and the butterfly represents times of elevation and advancement. Each Ministry is a God-given assignment designed to help establish the Kingdom of God. We are characterized by our spiritual tenacity to demonstrate the power of God, and to see that power operating in the life of the Believer. We invite you to embrace your Divine Assignment!

'The Kingdom has Come!'

Dr. Glories Powell, Th.D.

TABLE OF CONTENTS

CODA MINISTRIES

For the Lord God is a sun and shield; The Lord will give grace and glory;
No good thing will He withhold from those who walk upright.' (Psa. 84:11)

CODA, CHURCH OF DIVINE APPOINTMENT, (CALLED, ORDAINED, DEDICATED & ANOINTED), began in 1995 as an assignment placed in the heart of Dr. Glories Powell for a prison outreach program. It soon became evident that the prisoners were not only those behind physical bars but, men, women, and children in mental and spiritual prisons everywhere. By January 1, 2005, CODA Ministries was in a small office that could only seat about 30 people. These people were coming from all walks of life — from professionals to ex-drug addicts and everything in between. However, we were hungry for change.

Dr. Powell, and this small, intimate group of individuals, began to fulfill a God-given mandate that said, *'Raise an army for My Glory.'* This Divine instruction became the motivation for creating programs that taught revelation of Scripture, individual ministry development, a disciplined lifestyle of prayer and fasting… and much more. All of which would produce an army of focused, compelling and relevant men and women of God who would love and obey the Lord. They would be educated in the Word of GOD, anointed and skilled in the Prophetic; trained in Kingdom principles; and operating in each of the Seven Mountains of Culture. They would go beyond the walls of the church to serve God according to Matt. 25:31-41 which says, *"Feed the homeless, minister to the prisoner, visit the sick and help the orphaned."*

We practice the principle as stated by Thomas Aquinas, *"Preach the Gospel and use words if you have to."*

Dr. Powell, and faithful men and women have birthed a unique and amazing move of GOD… CODA MINISTRIES! We invite you to join us as we impact the community, the marketplace, and the Body of Christ with the manifestation of Him who has made us kings and priests unto God. To Him be Glory and Power forever!

What We Believe

We also believe, and therefore we speak! 2 Cor. 4:13

CODA MINISTRIES **(CALLED ORDAINED DEDICATED & ANOINTED)** and its Members, accept the following as the fundamental basis of belief:

• We believe the Bible to be the inspired Word of God, the infallible Word of God, and that the Bible is the only God-given authority that man possesses; therefore, all doctrine, faith, hope, and all instruction for the Believer must be based upon, and in harmony with, the Bible.

• We believe in the eternal Godhead who has revealed Himself as ONE God existing in three manifestations: Father, Son, and Holy Spirit; INDIVISIBLE. (Matt. 28:19; 2 Cor. 13:14)

• We believe sinners are saved by grace through repentance and faith in the perfect and FINISHED work of CHRIST, by His death, burial, and His resurrection from the dead.

• We believe in water baptism by immersion, in the Name of the Lord Jesus Christ, therefore fulfilling the command of Christ.
(Matt. 28:19; Acts 2:34-39, 10:47-48, 19:1-6; Luke 24:37)

• We believe in the baptism of the Holy Spirit subsequent to salvation, with the Scriptural evidence of speaking with other tongues as the Spirit gives utterance. (Acts 2:1-4, 4:14-17, 10:44-46; Gal. 3:14-15)

• We believe that we are a chosen generation, a royal priesthood, a holy nation, a peculiar people; and that we are citizens of the Kingdom of God, who have been called out of darkness into His marvelous light.

• We believe that the biblical form of Kingdom government is theocratic. Our leaders are ordained by confirmation of the Holy Spirit. And, our Pastor is under Apostolic authority and is qualified by the call of God, by a consecrated life, with Godly character, and the ability to rule.

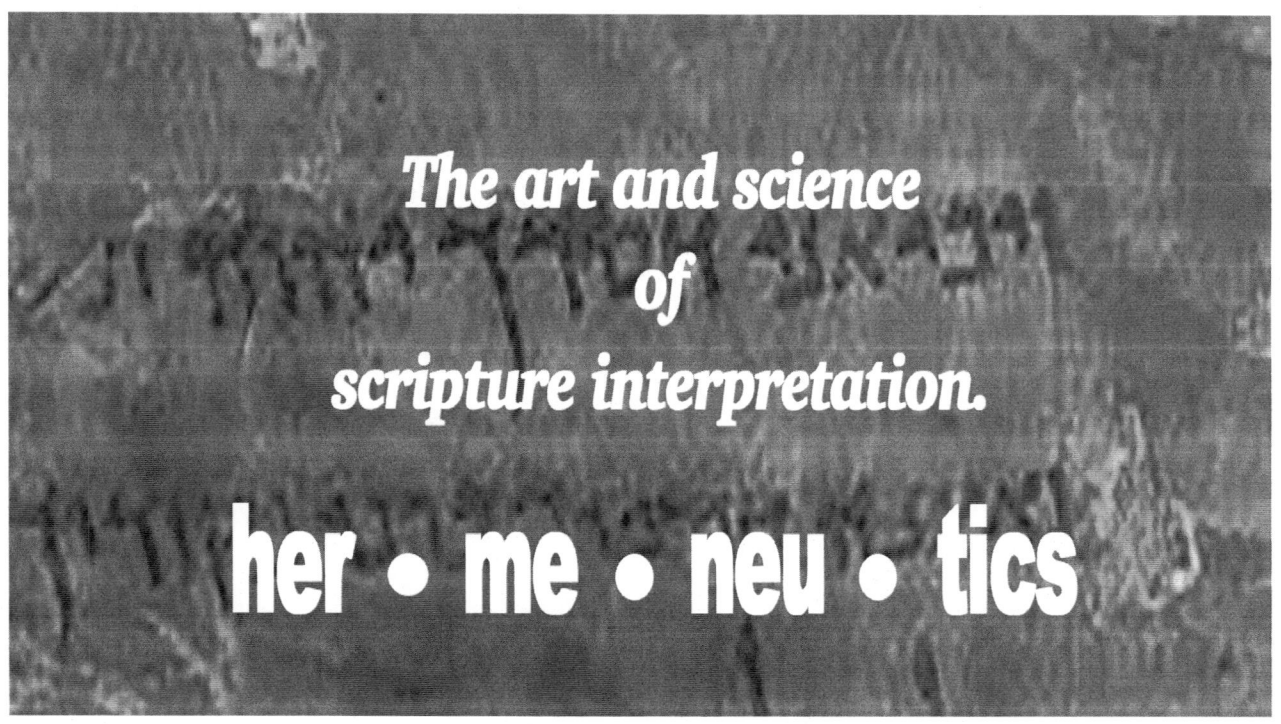

The art and science
of
scripture interpretation.

her • me • neu • tics

HERMENEUTICS

INTRODUCTION TO HERMENEUTICS

FIVE PHASES OF INTERPRETATION

FIVE COMMON CONCEPTS OF THEOLOGY

SIX STEPS OF TEXTUAL EXEGESIS

'But avoid foolish questions, and genealogies, and contentions, and strivings about the law; for they are unprofitable and vain.'   *Titus 3:9   (KJV)*

BIBLICAL HERMENEUTICS

'Study to show thyself approved unto God, a workman that need not to be ashamed, rightly dividing the word of truth.' 2 Tim. 2:15

Biblical Hermeneutics is the art and science of Scripture interpretation. It attempts to teach how to determine the meaning of the text to the original audience. Very often you hear people say, *'Just read the Bible and do what it says.'* The problem is that different people, even though they read the same Bible, often come to very different conclusions about what it actually says! The Christian Post recently published the findings of a Gallup poll designed to gauge Americans' opinion on the Bible. The findings reveal the chaos in our culture regarding the nature and authority of Scripture:

'Gallup's poll found that only 28 percent of Americans believe that the Bible is the Word of God and should be taken literally. And yet nearly 50 percent believe that the Bible is the 'inspired Word of God' while insisting that not all of its content be taken literally, but rather as metaphors and allegories that allow for interpretation.

The Bible is far more than a collection of metaphors and allegories. It is the written record of GOD's revelation of who He is, and ultimately, who we are in Him. This brief treatment of the subject can in no way address or teach every facet of biblical hermeneutics. Nor does this synopsis claim to provide all that you need to become well versed in the subject. However, after reading this study, you will be able to identify terms relevant to the principles of Biblical Studies and Hermeneutics. And, after applying these principles, you will be better able to approach the sacred writ with accuracy rightly dividing the Word of Truth.

The task of actually conveying an authentic interpretation of Scripture is overwhelming for many under-educated ministers today. Many are being influenced by the on-going lineup of personalities paraded daily on Christian television programs, while others are trying to seek an understanding of the Scriptures on their own with little or no training. This is dangerous. We are definitely living in times described in Matt. 24 by Christ Jesus speaking of the last days. We're living in perilous times. And, it's certainly not time for spiritual novices producing erroneous doctrine, stemming from erroneous interpretation of

Scripture. As you can see, the survival of the Church is contingent upon the power of the Truth being preached! That truth must be able to dispel darkness. It must be able to strengthen GOD's people against deception and being mislead by false doctrine. And, it must be able to compel a sin-sick world to believe in the LORD Jesus Christ! We cannot help but agree with Leonard Ravenhill[1] when he wrote:

"The tragedy of this late hour is that we have too many dead men in the pulpits giving out too many dead sermons to too many dead people." "Preaching is a spiritual business. A sermon born in the head reaches the head; a sermon born in the heart reaches the heart!"

It is imperative that we preach, as well as study, the Bible with an accurate understanding of how to correctly interpret Scripture. Hermeneutics is often called exegesis. However, they are not the same. Bernard Ramm said...

"Hermeneutics stands in the same relationship to exegesis that a rule-book stands to a game. The rules are not the game, and the game is meaningless without the rules. Hermeneutics proper is not exegesis, but exegesis is applied hermeneutics."[2]

There are two ancient schools of interpretation that we use today, the Allegorical from Alexandria in Egypt, which leans toward allegories and symbolism.And the Literal interpretation from Antioch in Greece, which leaned more toward the literal or maybe "letteral" (focused on spelling of words) hermeneutical approach. It focuses on the plain, obvious, ordinary, common sense meaning of words and sentences.

Scripture proves itself to be written not only allegorically and literally, but pneumatological (spiritually) as well. It is important that we understand that interpretation involves **spirit, soul, and body.**

'All Scripture is given by inspiration of God, and is profitable for doctrine, for reproof, for correction, for instruction in righteousness: That the man of God may be perfect, throughly furnished unto all good works.' 2 Tim. 3:16-17

---

[1] Leonard Ravenhill "Why Revival Tarries" by Bethany House Publishers August 1st 2004

[2]Utley, R. J. D. (1996). You Can Understand the Bible! (p. 25).

FIVE STAGES OF INTERPRETATION

Accurately interpreting Scripture is not limited to Bible scholars. It is the responsibility of every Believer to know how to use the tools necessary to understand what the text is saying. Rightly dividing the Word of GOD is essential to understanding the Mind of God. **In fact, if you cannot correctly interpret Scripture, it will be impossible to know the Will of God for your life through His Word.** This is what hermeneutics is all about.

There are five stages of Scripture interpretation. Each stage will provide information that will take you deeper into the search. You can't get lost! This process will help you become familiar with the terminology and principles used in the study of hermeneutics. You must provide the motivation and interest. The Holy Spirit will give you the understanding. The five stages of interpretation are: **Identify, Investigate, Introspect, Introduce and Implement.**[1]

1. Identify

You must first identify the genres (***kinds of literature***) by asking the question: In what category of literature does the text belong? ***Remember: the Bible is written both pneumatological*** (God's perspective) ***and phenomenological*** (man's perspective). Each literary genre has a different rule of interpretation.

Here are brief descriptions of the different genres found in Scripture:

- ***Historical Narratives*** - The narratives describe actual historical events from God's and man's perspective. They tell us what God is like (His character and nature), what God likes/dislikes, how He deals with people who obey and honor Him, and those who disobey and hate Him. Narratives give us principles and lessons. Historical Narratives are in Genesis, Exodus, Deuteronomy, Joshua, Judges, Ruth, 1-2 Samuel, 1-2 Kings, 1-2 Chronicles, Ezra, Nehemiah, and Esther. In the New Testament, you can find them in parts of the Gospels and the Acts.

---

[1] "Hermeneutics Practical Rules for Biblical Interpretation." 2017

- **Poetry and Songs -** These are expressions of emotion to God. They tell of feelings of happiness, joy, trust, hope, security, as well as feelings of discouragement, guilt, suffering, fear, anger, despair and repentance. Many of the songs were written for ceremonial temple worship and feast days. The Psalms were actually five books by several authors. In the Old Testament, these writings are found primarily in the Psalms, Song of Songs, and Job.

- **The Law (legal) Writings -** These writings indicate God's righteous standard, His idea of justice, principles of government, principles of health and safety, and His pattern and order of worship. The Law of Moses is NOT directly meant to be legalistic instructions or commands to Believers. But, the Law of the Covenant is as true today as it was in historical times. The legal writings are in Exodus, Leviticus, Numbers and Deuteronomy.

- **Wisdom Writings -** These writings reflect God's view of wisdom as opposed to man's view. They contain wise sayings and practical advice on how to live life and avoid trouble and hardship. Wisdom literature can be found primarily in Proverbs, Ecclesiastes and Job.

- **Prophecy -** 'The speaking forth of the mind and counsel of God' (pro 'forth' and phemi 'to speak') particularly prediction. It is the foretelling of future events, including declarations, exhortations, and warnings spoken by the prophets while acting under Divine influence. Prophecy is found throughout the Old Testament. However, they are the more difficult genres to interpret.

- **Gospels -** These writings tell of the birth, life, death, and resurrection of Jesus Christ. They contain statements of Christ concerning the nature and character of God, the Kingdom of God/Heaven, what God expects of us, principles of righteous living, and the ways in which Yeshua fulfilled the OT prophecies. These books are Matthew, Mark, Luke, and John.

- **Parables -** Parables are stories with parallel meanings. Parables are illustrative and provocative. They are designed to draw people in with a familiar or natural example that is placed alongside a spiritual principle. Most parables have only one message or central idea, and even if there are multiple messages, one will be the main idea. Parables are primarily found in the Gospels.

- **Letters -** The letters are generally documents written with a clear purpose to an identified audience. However, some letters (called epistles) were written to circulate to a larger group. The letter/epistle writer presents arguments to correct, rebuke, defend, instruct, praise, and encourage their readers. Letters/epistles are the majority of the New Testament from Acts to Jude.

- **Apocalypse -** This word means to 'uncover or reveal.' It includes the book of Revelation and parts of Ezekiel and Daniel. Revelation is the testimony of Jesus Christ, a prophetic warning and encouragement to the seven churches, and prophetic visions for Believers past, present, and future.

2. Investigate

The three most important factors in exegesis (extracting the meaning from the text) are context, context and context. Understanding the context is the key to understanding what the text underlined meant to the original audience. Your investigation should discover the **original intent** of the biblical text in its **correct** context. There are two aspects of contextual analysis:

- **Historical Context -** The Bible was **written** over a period of time dating from approximately 2000 BC (Job) to 95 AD. The historical/cultural context will tell what, when, where, and how a subject was being addressed. Consult Bible dictionaries, encyclopedias and Bible handbooks to read about manners, customs and historical background of various nations.

- **Literary Context -** The literary context is an inductive approach to trace the thought development of a book (discovered via exegetical research). It determines what the Scripture addressed in its context. Why is the text in this position? Why is it in the Bible at all? What difference would it make if it were left out?

3. Introspect - Pray!

Without introspection you would only look at the passage as it applies to others. It is vitally important to realize what the passage means to you first. Introspection comes through prayer and meditation.

- *Prayer* - Prayer will open your spirit and enable you, by the leading of the Holy Spirit, to see the entire picture as opposed to a fragmented view of the text. Prayer also allows the Holy Spirit an opportunity to give you revelation and insights concerning the mind of GOD and the hidden meaning in the passage.

- *Meditation* – Meditation does not mean emptying your head of everything. It means filling your mind with all the information required to make decisions about what the text says. Allow the Holy Spirit to give you understanding of how significant the text is to your life, and how it should be applied to today. The minister should pray and meditate throughout the entire interpretive process, not only when you are about to deliver your message.

4. Introduce Data

- What does a particular key word or phrase mean? Pay attention to the elements that are repeated in a particular passage or used elsewhere by the same author.

- Does the word/phrase carry any special significance given the historical/ cultural context? What does it contribute to the overall meaning of the text?

- How would the meaning of the text be affected if this particular word/ phrase was left out?

- Is there a progression in the story, account or argument? Is there a climax?

Determine the relationships between key words and phrases. Especially look for the following connecting words:

Contrast	but, however, even though, much more, nevertheless, yet, although, then, otherwise
Condition	if, whoever, whatever
Comparison	too, also, as, just as, so also, likewise, like, in the same way
Correlatives	as...so also, for...as, so...as
Reason	because, for this reason, for this purpose, for, since
Result	so then, therefore, as a result, thus, then
Purpose	that, so that, in order that
Time	now, immediately, just then, until, when, before, after, while, during, since
Geographic	where, from

5. Implement

To implement means to *'put in practice.'* After you complete the hermeneutical research, the following questions should be asked:

- Is there a command to obey?

- Is there an error to avoid?

- Does the passage point out sinful behavior or attitudes that may be present in your own life?

- Is there an example to follow?

- Is there a promise to claim?

- Does the passage highlight an aspect of God's nature and character which you had not seen before?

To implement the text means to become more than a hearer of the Word, but a doer also. Implementation is necessary for teaching others how to apply the precepts of GOD.

SIX STEPS TO TEXTUAL EXEGESIS

Using this six-step procedure, you will analyze the text to derive an accurate interpretation of its relevance for our lives today. In this analytical process, we will use six different modes of transportation. Each step will take you closer to an accurate interpretation, and finally personal application. Imagine that you are trying to get to a house located in the woods. We will begin with the Theological analysis (the airplane), since higher elevation gives a greater range of visibility. Next, Contextual analysis (the helicopter), provides a closer view of yet a broader range of sight. Then Historical/Cultural (the automobile), let us see social background roads and trails leading to our destination. Next, Lexical/Syntax (the bicycle), brings us to those tight areas of the context of words and how they relate to each other. And finally, Exegesis, where we're on foot and able to extract the **exact meaning** of each word in the text. When we have made a complete and accurate analysis, we can provide an accurate application of the biblical principle to our lives and arrive at our ultimate destination … the mind of GOD!

1. Theological Analysis (Airplane)

Theology is the study of (the Mind) of God and how He relates to His creation. The theological analysis reveals how the passage fits into the entire pattern of GOD's relationship to man, and the revelation of GOD's plan of salvation. What does the text tell about the revelation of the plan of GOD? Where does the text fall on the timeline of the unveiling of GOD's relationship to man? Theological analysis becomes significant when comparing the Book of the Covenant vs. the Book of the Law; or the study of Righteousness, the Cross, the Melchizedek Priesthood, angelic and demonic activity and how these principles developed over time. There are two major schools of thought on GOD's salvation plan.

Continuity - Those who understand salvation history as primarily continuous generally view <u>all Scripture</u> as relevant for the believer today.

Discontinuity - Those who view salvation history as primarily discontinuous view only the Book of Acts and the Epistles as primarily relevant for the Church today.

Five Common Concepts of Theology

1) **No Theology** - believes that Scripture is man's thoughts about GOD, and is an evolutionary history of Israel's religion.

2) **Dispensational Theory** - Primary emphasis on discontinuity. Scofield defines a dispensation as *"a period of time during which man is tested in respect of obedience to some specific revelation of the will of GOD."* The pattern of salvation history is three-fold. GOD gives man a pattern for obedience; Man fails; GOD responds with a grace and a different dispensation of responsibility. For example: Innocence, Conscience, Civil Government, Promise, Mosaic Law, Grace, and Millennium are dispensations according to Scofield and others.

3) **Lutheran Theory** - believes that we must distinguish between two parallel and present truths throughout Scripture: Law and Gospel

4) **Covenantal Theology** - focuses on continuity. The belief is that all biblical history is covered by two covenants: a covenant of works from the fall to the cross, and a covenant of grace from the cross to the present.

5) **Epigenetic Model** - views Divine revelation as analogous to the growth of a tree from a seed, to a seedling, to a young tree, and then to a fully grown tree. The term is not widely used and is referred to as the organic unity of Scripture. The epigenetic theory sees GOD's self disclosures as never being imperfect or errant, even though later disclosures may add further information. This 'Progressive' revelation is the concept that GOD's revelation gradually increased in definiteness, clarity, and understanding as it was revealed over time!

2. Contextual Analysis (Helicopter)

The study of scripture is never complete until you move from text to context. Contextualization answers these questions: What issue is being addressed? What is the genre? Who is speaking to whom? Grant Osborne in his book *'Hermeneutical Spiral'* wrote, *"The second stage in serious Bible study is to consider the larger context within which a passage is found. We must understand the whole before attempting to dissect the parts. Two areas must be considered at the beginning of Bible study: the historical context and the logical context.*

Under the first category we study introductory material on the biblical book in order to determine the situation to which the book was addressed. Under the second category we use an inductive approach in order to trace the thought development of a book. Both aspects are necessary before we begin a detailed analysis of a particular passage.[1]

a. Look at the outline of the book. What is the major block of verses and how do they fit as a whole? (Consider the different outline of the book of Proverbs.)

b. Determine the logical grouping. What is being said before and after the verse? This is called the 1, 2, 3-1 rule. Read the verse before the text and the verse following the text, then read the first verse of that chapter. See if the passage contributes to the author's argument. Never begin contextual analysis in the middle of a sentence even if it means starting at the beginning of another verse. Your primary focus is to get an accurate understanding of the concept of the text. Remember that Scripture cannot mean what it has never meant.

c. Determine the perspective of the author. Distinguish between descriptive and prescriptive truth. Is he describing a situation or is he prescribing? There are one of three voices speaking in any Scripture: when man speaks it may or may not be true; when Satan speaks it is a mixture of truth and lies; or when God is speaking it's all truth! When Scripture describes a human action without comment, it should not be assumed that God approves the action.

d. Distinguish between incidental details, and erroneous conclusions. i.e., *(The prodigal son didn't need a mediator, other than the prayers of His father, so we don't need one!)* This is a common result of poor contextual analysis. Stay focused on the text. Keep the main thing the main thing.

e. Determine who is being addressed in the passage. The angel Gabriel was talking to Mary, not you! *Every promise in the Bible is NOT yours.* Promises and commands are usually directed to either national Israel, Old Testament believers, or New Testament believers.

---

[1]Osborne, Grant R. (2010-02-25). The Hermeneutical Spiral: A Comprehensive Introduction to Biblical Interpretation (Kindle Locations 480-484).

3. Historical-Cultural analysis (Automobile)

The meaning of a text cannot be interpreted with certainty without looking into the historical-cultural analysis. The primary and most important question to ask is, 'What does this text mean to the original writer and his audience?'

a. What is the <u>general</u> historical milieu (environment) in which the writer speaks? In other words, what was the political, economic, and social situation? What were the major threats and concerns? You can find this information within the book, or with outside historical data. (commentaries, dictionaries, etc.)

b. What knowledge of certain customs would clarify the meaning of a passage? (Example: *How would Sarah have a son through Hagar? What is corban?*)

c. What is the <u>specific</u> historical-cultural context and purpose of this book? For instance:

Who was the writer? (*Apostle, farmer, prophet*)

What was his spiritual background and experience? *(Luke never met Jesus)*

To whom was he writing? (*Jews, gentiles, believers in danger of becoming apostate?*)

What was the writer's purpose in writing this particular book? *(his intention) Look for repetitive phrase; see the hortatory part of his writing (hortai= to encourage, incite, urge).* <u>This information is generally found in the outline of the book</u>. A good way to check whether you understand the author's purpose is to summarize his purpose in a single sentence.

4. Lexical-Syntactical Analysis (Bicycle)

Lexical-Syntactical analysis is the study of the meaning of individual words (lexicology) and the way those words are combined (syntax), in order to determine more accurately the author's intended meaning. Lexical-Syntactical analysis recognizes when an author intends his words to be understood literal, or figuratively, or symbolically and then interprets them accordingly. So, when Jesus said, *"I am the door," "I am the wine," and "I am the bread of life,"* we understand these expressions to be metaphors, as he intended. When He said,

"Be on your guard against the yeast of the Pharisees and Sadducees," He intended yeast to be symbolic of their false teachings. (Matt. 16) When He said to the paralytic, *"Get up, take your mat and go home,"* He expected the paralyzed man to literally obey His command which the man did. (Matt. 9:6)

<u>Lexical syntactical analysis is founded on the premise that although words may take on a variety of meanings in different contexts, they have but one intended meaning in any given context</u>. If I were to say, *'He is green.'* These words might mean that: *(1) he is inexperienced (2) he looks sick (3) he is envious*. Although the words could mean any of these three things, the context usually will indicate which of these ideas we wish to communicate. Lexical-syntactical analysis is needed because, without it our interpretation would not be any more valid than that of any heretical group. The steps for lexical syntactical analysis are:

a. <u>Identify the general literary</u> form (prose, poetry, prophecy, etc.) which will influence the way the author intended his words to be understood.

b. <u>Identify the natural division</u> of the text which is the transitional statements and conceptual units that make the authors thought process clearer.

c. <u>Identify the connecting words</u> (conjunctions, prepositions, relative pronouns) that show the relationship between two or more thoughts.

d. <u>Determine what an individual word</u> means. A word that's used for a long time in a language begins to take on a variety of meanings. So it is necessary to determine which one of the several possible meanings the author intended to convey in a specific context.

e. <u>Analyze the syntax</u>. The relationship of words to one another is expressed through their grammatical forms and arrangement.

f. <u>Write the results</u> of your analysis in non-technical, easily understood words that clearly convey the author's meaning.

5. Exegesis (Foot) Etymology

To Exegete the text means to extract the meaning. This term is used to define hermeneutics in general, and specifically in finding the definition of each word in the text. On foot, you will define each word from the original language in both Greek or Hebrew. A Strong's concordance and an Interlinear Bible can be very helpful in exegesis. Understanding textual criticism is important here because the interpreters will often insert a word (in italics) that is not in the original text. Definitions are to be taken from a Bible lexicon and not Webster's dictionary.

6. Principlizing (Relevance)

Principlizing means to discover the spiritual, moral, or theological principles and show their relevance for believers today. It is based on the premise that the Holy Spirit chose the incidents written in Scripture for a reason whether to make a point, give information, or illustrate a truth. **Principlizing** is a method of conveying a truth in such a way that we can recognize the original reason it was included in Scripture, the principles it was meant to teach, and how it relates to us today. The method or approach is the same as in any exegetical process.

1. You carefully look at the cultural customs or the historical circumstances that may illuminate the significance of various actions.

2. Determine the purpose of the book that contains the text.

3. Determine the contextual analysis.

4. Determine the theological analysis.

Following these steps will allow you to analyze the narrative and articulate how the principles can be used for the believer today.[1] This is a journey we must take across the barriers of time, culture, language, and customs —if we are to rightly divide the word of Truth. (2 Tim 2:15)

---

[1] J. Scott Duvall and J. Daniel Hays 'Grasping God's Word' 2004

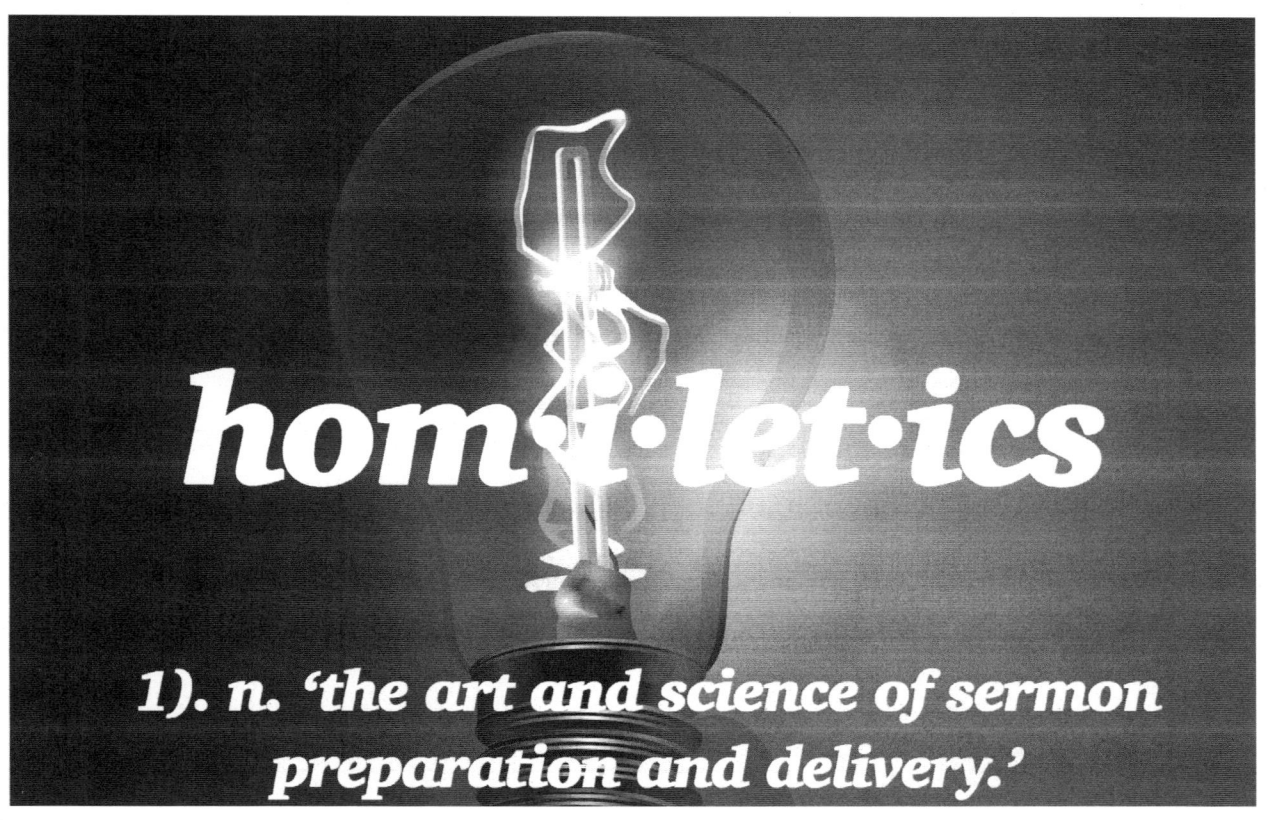

1). n. 'the art and science of sermon preparation and delivery.'

HOMILETICS

SERMON PREPARATION

SERMON OUTLINE

SERMON INTRODUCTIONS

SERMON DESIGNS

PREACHING ETIQUETTE

Preach the word; be instant in season, out of season; reprove, rebuke, exhort with all long suffering and doctrine. 2 Tim. 4:2

HOMILETICS

Preach the word; be instant in season, out of season; reprove, rebuke, exhort with all long suffering and doctrine. Titus 4:2

This brief outline is taken from my book "The Art and Science of Biblical Homiletics,"[1] a handbook on the subject of sermon preparation and delivery. Homiletics is an art because it is a skill acquired by experience, study and observation. The art of preaching allows for creative expression. Each preacher must bring to their sermon their own personal creativity and experiences. The art of homiletics is clearly seen in the styles and methods that preachers have developed over the years. No one can deliver a message from *your* spirit like you can. Science is knowledge that is built upon strong, logical premises which can be communicated and understood. Homiletics is a science because it has laws that govern its application and systematic research.

After more than 25 years of experience in ministry, with 12 years of pastoring and a doctorate in theology, I realized that I had learned enough to know that there was so much more to learn… especially in the field of Homiletics and Biblical Studies. Although it would be impossible to cover every facet of Biblical Homiletics, I have endeavored to share from my studies a list of research techniques, sermon designs, methods of delivery and examples of sermon outlines. As the Apostle Paul said to Timothy, *'study to show thyself approved a workman before God, rightly dividing the word if truth.' (2 Tim. 2:15)* So must we study and apply ourselves to adequately present the message of the Kingdom in the midst of a perverse generation. I thank God for the opportunity to gain knowledge in this field, but expertise alone is not enough. I pray that it will be evident that my experience involves more than a mere academic discipline. A preacher must live their message. We must allow the Holy Spirit to work through us and expect the power of God's Word to change lives. It gives me great pleasure to sow into the lives of individuals who are seeking to become skilled in presenting the Word of God.

---

[1] Dr. Glories Powell "The Art and Science of Biblical Homiletics" 2011

Eight Steps to Sermon Preparation

Step 1. DETERMINE THE PURPOSE - Why are you preaching? What's this occasion? What do you want the people to do, or understand, as a result of hearing your message? Purpose defines boundaries. This information comes from the theme of a conference, a speaking invitation, or a special occasion. The 'purpose' of the sermon is also called the topic or theme, and the burden of the Lord.

Step 2. SEARCH THE Scripture - Read your Bible. Use a concordance and find a Scripture that supports and clearly relates to your purpose. Finding a Scripture is an important step and often difficult to nail down because there are so many Scriptures that may fit your subject, not to mention making the mistake of choosing a Scripture taken out of context. Sometimes the idea for a message comes before you have a Scripture. But, once you have a Scripture, your idea should be shaped by the content of the text. In other words, you don't have a sermon if you don't have a Scripture.

Step 3. COLLECT DATA - First, write down your thoughts on the subject, then gather information and write down every idea you have on a scratch pad. Use a concordance to look up keywords relating to your subject. Also, read various translations. Use reference books primarily word studies, dictionary, and Naves Topical index. Never attempt to get opinions from commentaries before you exhaust your thoughts and word studies, and remember to write them down!

Step 4. SELECT MAIN POINTS - Choose from the information on your notepad. I typically use three points because it helps to keep my delivery balanced. Use the points that best fit your purpose and your subject. Make sure they are related to and supported by Scriptures. Your challenge may be feeling limited and restricted by the text. But, when you begin to study the context of the text, and the situations surrounding it, you will discover a lot of relevant information for your subject. Start with the first point and work until you finish each point.

Step 5. STAY FOCUSED - Brainstorm on a legal pad with supporting points or statements. Constantly check your work against the purpose for your message. Discard everything that doesn't fit your purpose. Remember that the purpose of your message will give you clear boundaries. It also gives power and vision. So, don't dilute it with things that do not move your message forward with its purpose and impact.

Step 6. CHOOSE A DESIGN - Your design will help you determine what style of delivery will best facilitate the information that you've gathered, including illustrations, points and a call to action. You have a purpose and you should now ask the listeners to perform it. Give a directive to the people to take action, to do what you had in mind as you prepared the message. Don't be shy. The design you choose (if applied) will move you smoothly through transitions between points and help you present a clear call to action.

Step 7. ADD ILLUSTRATIONS - Now you want to illustrate your sermon. Seek out places in the message that a good story will make it clearer. A good illustration can make or break a supporting statement.

Step 8. WRITE THE INTRODUCTION - You cannot write an introduction until you have something to introduce. So, a good time to write the introduction is last. This is also a good time to shape your title if you have one. Titles are good for reference and as a hook to remember your Scripture or dominant thought.

Remember the wise words of Waldon Marsh, *'Learning how to preach and write sermons is sort of like learning to swim. You can read all the instructions and commit to memory all the techniques but you will never really learn how to preach until you practice.'*

SERMON OUTLINE

The outline is the typical order of any form of communication whether you are writing a letter, or making a phone call. The structure of the sermon outline is quite simple. The purpose of the sermon outline is to have notes that are easy to follow while you're preaching. Your notes should be arranged so that you can glance at them and recognize where you are in the message, unlike using a sermon manuscript where you can easily get lost when you take your eyes off of the page. I personally use the outline to rehearse my delivery. Many times writing an outline will give you a mental picture of the order and flow of your information. Sermon manuscripts (where you write everything out), do not allow for freedom of expression because each phrase is written exactly as you would say it, and to deviate may cause you to lose focus or become confused with the following words or paragraphs. Beginning preachers often start with writing manuscripts for fear of not remembering all the information in their message ... including the *'say Amen, somebody!'*

A sermon outline should be creative, easy to read with brief sentences at the same time, keeping the message transitioning from one point to another. The outline helps to organize your ideas, making it easy to see how they develop and connect to each other. The outline begins with your encounter of the text. It is the embryo of the message. There are six stages to a sermon outline.

The opening in a message includes the Greeting, Intro, and Thematic Statement. (It is also sometimes referred to as the introduction.)

Greeting – The greeting is mentioned in the sermon outline because it is the speaker's first statement. It's often the first impression of the speaker that an audience has. It is important because people have a tendency to determine whether they want to listen to you based upon how you present yourself in greeting the audience.

Introduction – The introduction *'introduces your topic.'* It gives the initial reason why your topic should be important and relevant to them, and why you are qualified to teach it. The introduction should capture the attention and make your message relevant to the listener.

7 Introductions:

- Declaration - To make a declaration of fact or truth about your topic.
- Testimony - A personal testimony pertaining to your topic.
- Question - Questions that will cause introspection and attention
- Illustration - A short story, parable or humorous (fitting) joke
- Quote - A quote from a reliable person relevant to your topic
- Historical - Gives the historical background of the text.
- Statistics - Credible Stats pertaining to your topic

Thematic Statement – What's the big idea? **A good thematic statement contains the big idea!** It is often called a thesis, or a statement of intent. A thematic statement is the concise and condensed presentation that **explains** the subject. It is the **central idea**. The word 'theme' is from the Greek *thema,* "a proposition, subject, deposit," literally "*something set down.*" The word 'idea' itself moved into English from the Greek word *'idein'* which means 'to see' and therefore 'to know.' An idea sometimes enables us to see what was previously unclear. The thematic statement should 'set down' the subject and describe the general meaning of the topic, not the specific events, actions, or characters. It should not be so general that it says nothing…and yet not be so involved that it says too much without explanation. It is specific and focused. The thematic statement contains the:

- **The Problem -** The issue to be addressed. (make it a real problem)
- **The Consequences -** Situations resulting from the problem.
- **The Solution -** What Scripture gives as answers to the problem.

The Body – The body of your message consists primarily of the explanation, interpretation, and application of a single dominant idea, supported by other ideas, drawn from one passage, or several passages of Scripture. It answers, with clarity, the questions who, what, when, where, and how. It is where you 'develop' what you have declared (in the thematic statement) and established as the dominant thought in the text. The body is where you develop the main points of the message.

The Design constructs the body of the message.

10 Designs

- Categorical
- Numeric
- Spacial
- Sequential
- Expository
- Exegetical
- Contrast and Comparison
- Character
- Topical
- Textual

Summary – The summary reiterates the thematic statement. It should also contain the solution to the problem and/or questions that were posed in the opening. The summary reiterates the speaker's main points. It should be creative and enlightening. The summary should be delivered in a slightly different way than the thematic statement, but saying the same thing. *It tells them what you told them.*

Close – The close gives the audience information that will trigger their minds to remember the heart of the message. *It tells them again!* If there is a call to action, the instruction should be easy to follow. Too many closing details can cause your message to sound fragmented and unfinished. **To deliver what has not been promised is boring. To promise what is not delivered is cruel.** So, the whole matter of the end of the sermon is related to the movement of the sermon, and the movement of the sermon should carry a sense of an ending. Remember, to close means to close!

THE INTRODUCTION

The introduction gains attention, interest, establishes credibility, and previews the main idea of the message. Most people are poor listeners, and even good listeners need all the help they can get in sorting out a speaker's points and ideas. You can help your listeners by telling them in the introduction what they should listen for in the rest of the message. It is said that your audience makes strong assumptions about you during the first eight to ten minutes of your message. For this reason you need to start strong and launch a clear topic. Focus your efforts on completing this task after developing the central idea (the thematic statement) of the message.

The introduction should capture the interest of the audience. It should leave the audience feeling a need and a desire to hear more. It should make them feel as if you are qualified to give them information concerning the subject. In addition to the knowledge you have about the text, you also need to consider the terminology you want to use. Most messages have specific terminologies that your audience may or may not be familiar with, especially when you are preaching from a parable, a psalm, or a prophecy.

A message may contain a combination of introductions. However, you must be careful not to become redundant by introducing the topic in too many ways before getting to your point.
The introduction should also comply with the type of design you choose. For example, if you use a spatial design, you would probably not want to use an illustration for an introduction.

<u>When assessing your audience, you must ask the following questions</u>:

1. What is the purpose of the message? (an exhortation, worship service, seminar, funeral, special program, etc.)
2. What are the ages, gender, or levels of education of my primary audience?
3. What level of information will they have on the subject?
4. How familiar are they with the text(s)?

The Purpose of the Introduction

Introduce the topic-

Too often preachers make the mistake of waiting to 'drop the bomb' and end up introducing their main idea too late into the message.   By then, your central point looks like one of many thoughts. However, when you let the people in on where you're going from the beginning, and they know what your subject is going to be, there is a good chance they will stay with you throughout the message. A typical 'faux pas' in preaching is to drag the introduction too far into the body of your message. The audience could become bored and disinterested because of a slow start with much speaking. You should make the introduction brief and no more than 10 to 20 percent of your message.   A practical introduction will whet the appetite and pique the interest of the audience. Typically, you state the topic of your message in the introduction. People tend to relax when they are comfortable with your presentation. Preachers who present their topic during the opening are more likely to have a stronger impact on the audience. Elaborate and repeat it often. Even when your audience know what your topic is before you begin, you should state it clearly and concisely in the introduction.

Prepare the audience-

Any information is filtered through a listener's frame of reference – the total of his or her knowledge, experiences, goals, values, and attitudes.   You may have people in your audience with different frames of reference, so in order to be effective, it's important that the listener agrees that the message is for them and not only for their neighbor. However, you shouldn't spend two thirds of your message trying to convince the listeners that they need to hear what you have to say. Your introduction should pique their interest. Qualifying your audience means to strategically convince them that your message will be interesting and relevant. Gaining their attention and interest can be done by asking questions or giving an inspiring testimony. Get their attention by startling your listeners with statistics, or a graphic illustration. Any of the seven introductions that will be covered in this section will help you impact your audience. Remember, people pay attention to things that directly affect them.

Qualify the Speaker-

You have very little time to engage the interest of today's audiences. With the tremendous influx of information on the internet and other forms of media, people are less tolerant with an unqualified teacher (or preacher), so your opening is a good place to demonstrate your knowledge and ability concerning your topic. There is nothing more disheartening than someone who obviously doesn't have a handle on what they are speaking about. An articulate and informative introduction will give your audience confidence that you are qualified to speak on the subject.

Never introduce the introduction!   Stick to the action and avoid opening sentences with phrases like these:

- It is my opinion that …
- The point I wish to make is that …
- The Lord is leading me to go another way, so …
- I would like to introduce this message by saying …

Again, 'never introduce the introduction!'
"Nike" which reminds us to 'just do it!' In this case 'Just say it'.

A good introduction prepares the audience for the subject. Your knowledge on the subject does not have to be based on firsthand experience. It can come from reading, from courses that you've taken, or from people that you've met. Just remember to inform the audience of your source and give credit where credit is due. Credibility, on the other hand, is different. Your character speaks louder than your message.

It may be difficult to convince your audience that you have a godly lifestyle if your reputation contradicts it. Your lifestyle will always preach louder than your messages. Thomas Aquinas once wrote, *"Preach the Gospel and use words if you must."*

SEVEN TYPES OF INTRODUCTIONS

Declaration

Making a declaration has the ability to get the immediate attention of your audience. Whether it is the 'shock and awe' consequences of sin, or a Biblical mandate… the declaration must be theologically sound, biblically correct and culturally relevant. It must also be true! You cannot build an argument on a point that is biblically incorrect and theologically unfounded. A declaration is an in-the-face approach to introducing a topic, or making a point, and is generally used with ethos and logos as opposed to pathos. In other words, it doesn't usually appeal to the emotions, but rather it challenges the intellect. A declaration normally deals with the facts.

Historical

A historical introduction is used when you want to give background information. It will explain an event in biblical history. (i.e., the tabernacle, the fall of Adam, the conversion of Paul, etc.) You can also use the historical introduction if your message is teaching doctrine. However, beware of too much information, because your audience could get bogged down and lose interest before you get to the thematic statement. Just be careful not to get so wrapped up in the background that you forget your dominant thought. The historical or background introduction is also effective to connect a series of messages on a particular subject. It is equivalent to recapping the main point of the previous message and using the information as an introduction. Caution, you should always explain the historical context as well. (Lots of information).

Illustration

An illustration is a short story. This type of introduction is particularly effective in a persuasive message. It allows the speaker to use vivid word pictures and descriptions that will appeal to the senses and emotions of the audience. Because of the different literacy needs, the audience should be able to engage multiple modalities. An introduction with an illustration will cause them to feel, see, think, or experience excitement, horror or delight. The audience will become sensitive to the burden (or the dominant thought) early in the message (which is what you want). The more vivid the detail, the more sympathetic the audience will be to your cause. You will need to support your claims with whatever facts, but the emotional appeal of the short descriptive narrative will make your audience more receptive to what you have to say.

Question

An introduction with a question is effective for making the audience think about your topic. If the question is vague and irrelevant, the audience will most likely respond to it in the same way. Asking a question (or series of questions), is a simple and common way of engaging the audience. Questions (normally) automatically make the listener assess whether the subject is relevant, and/or whether they would be interested in hearing more of the message.

Quote

When you quote, you generally want to be as concise as possible. Only use the part that is strictly relevant to your own point. Quoting notable, powerful words of writers or other famous people can prove to be an effective way to get attention. It's also impressive because, when you use the credibility of one that has the reputation, knowledge, or experience, it also enhances your credibility. Using a quotation can also help to connect the audience with the personality of the person you're quoting. By the same token, use caution when you introduce your topic with a quote from someone that is unfamiliar.

Statistic

A preacher is always faced with the challenge of making their audience see the relevance of their message. Using a shocking statistic can open the minds of the audience to the possibility of tragedy hitting home, and that will make them more receptive to your message. People don't normally believe that a crisis situation or devastation will happen to them. But, an alarming statistic will change their minds. For example, stating that, "4 billion people have been diagnosed with HIV"… is startling. However, stating that, "1 in every 4 young adults will be diagnosed HIV positive"… is a much more personally relevant statistic. Please remember that statistics must be reputable and factual!

Testimony

Your testimony in the introduction will give credibility. And, it will draw more attention to your delivery. People are always interested to see how you physically or mentally handled whatever you're speaking about. Inquiring minds want to know. A testimony, unlike other illustrations, cannot be used often, because it will become predictable. Use your testimony carefully and sparingly.

As you look over the various ways of introducing your subject, take a mental note of where you would use logos (logic), ethos (credibility) or pathos (emotion), or a combination of the three.

Points to remember in preparing your introduction:
- Work on your introduction after you have prepared the body of your message.
- Try several introductions to see how they blend with your message.
- Keep the introduction short and sweet. 10% to 15% of the message.
- Never use terminology that introduces the introduction. NIKE!

Sermon Designs

The design is the body of the message. Any well balanced message will contain an introduction and a thematic statement, but the sermon design is determined by the method of delivery. This will keep him/her 'process-oriented' as the pulpit work is anticipated and planned.

James Massey said in his work 'Designing the Sermon,'[1] *"Any sermon worth hearing will grow out of a heart and head whose feeling and thought have been projected toward some clear end to which the speaking will move."*

"An effective design will have a point to make, an idea to express, a scene to share, a cause to promote, a doctrine to set forth and apply, an action to inspire, a feeling to arouse, a direction to point out, a divine promise to share, a caution to give, a person to claim."

The preacher must be a designer to achieve the goals of the gospel and handle the job with competence. The design (the body of the message) is essential for shaping what one intends to deliver. This means that the sermon design should have a clear aim and logical structure.

Biologist C. M. Child wrote:
"Structure and function are mutually related. Function produces structure and structure modifies and determines the character of function."

The design of the body should be in a clear, concise format that is put in order for the sake of an experience. It is planned to make the 'hearing' a 'happening.' The design should have focus, balance, logical sequence, emphasis, strategic supporting material, (illustrations, examples, humor, etc.), and a calculated impact.

Each design has its own unique outline, allowing the message to be organized and thoroughly developed. Listed below are ten designs that give a variety of methods for sermon delivery.

---

[1] James Massey 'Designing the Sermon'

Categorical

The categorical design is normally used when you have a lot of information to cover. You should definitely use a categorical design for subjects that have natural or customary divisions. For example:

The four phases of Joseph's life-
1. The pit
2. Potiphar's house
3. The prison
4. The palace

The three phases of the prodigal son's story-
1. He rebelled
2. He repented
3. He returned

The three-fold process of Salvation-
1. Saved
2. Being Saved
3. Will be Saved

Preachers often make the mistake of overwhelming their audience with information. The categorical design helps the speaker organize the information to balance the delivery of the message. Each category should have its own main point. However, it is helpful if you open each category with the same wording. It also makes it easier for the audience to remember the main points and illustrations in the message. Try to keep the message between three and five categories, and make sure the thematic statement is addressed in the first and last category. Balancing the amount of time for each category is also important. You want to give each category enough time to be relevant and effective.

Introduction (Introduces the topic)
Thematic Statement (Introduce the categories)
  Body
I. Main point #1 (first category)   (Transition into main point 2)
II. Main point #2 (second category)   (Transition into main point 3)
III. Main point #3 (third category)   (Transition into conclusion)
Summary
Conclusion

Character

The character design basically spotlights the life of a biblical character. This design covers the character's station in life, their strengths, weaknesses, gifts, and personality traits, especially those that are most relevant to their spiritual development. David, Paul, Samson, Esther, Mary, Moses, Joseph (just to name a very few) are examples of the characters that many speakers use to show the power of the presence of God in the life of a believer. You must be able to make their characteristics relevant to your central idea, whether you're expressing their good traits, or negative personality traits. Your message is exemplifying a topic by using their personality or their experience with God. Remember, the topic of your message is more important than the personality traits of the biblical character. The main points in the message must not be overshadowed by information about the character. Either way, this design requires in-depth knowledge concerning the particular character.

Below is an example of the outline for the character design.

Introduction: Introduce the topic
Thematic Statement: (Introduce the character)
Body
I. Main point #1 (personality trait, situation, point)   (Transition)
II. Main point #2 (personality trait, situation, point)   (Transition)
III. Main point #3 (personality trait, situation, point) (Transition into conclusion)

Summary: Summarize the character traits and burden
Conclusion

Exegetical

The key to an exegetical design is to develop your topic using the definitions of each word in the passage. This requires some knowledge of lexical-syntactical analysis. You will need to understand how certain words relate to each other and how they have evolved etymologically. Exegesis is from a Greek word which means to 'lead out'. It is a critical explanation or interpretation of a text. The exegetical design defines, or draws out the meaning of each word in the text.

This design requires a Strong's concordance and a Greek or Hebrew lexicon (depending on the location of the text). In the exegetical design the message is developed as the text is developed. For example, if you use the exegetical design with James 1:3 it would read as follows:

'**...knowing this,** [allow, be aware (of), feel, (have) knowledge of, perceive, be resolved, be sure, understand] **that** [because (that), for (that), how (that), (in) that] **the trying** [dokimion- a testing; for trustworthiness: trial] **of your faith** [pistis- persuasion, credence, moral conviction (of) truth itself: - assurance, belief, believe, fidelity] **works** [to accomplish; to finish, fashion: - cause, perform] **patience** [hupomone- cheerful (or hopeful) endurance, constancy: - enduring patience, patient continuance (waiting)]

With the exegetical design you come to the text like a detective in a crime scene, examining all of the nuances of each word. Notice that the definition following each underlined word in the passage is amplified (including conjunctions and prepositions). While the meaning of the text is defined by its context, the message is being constructed by the amplified definitions of the words in the passage. Remember, the exegetical design pulls the meaning out of each word in the text, as opposed to eisegesis, where you introduce your own presuppositions, agendas, or biases into the text. The exegetical design can be very effective in teaching a deeper understanding of a familiar passage and for Scripture memory.

Introduction

Thematic Statement:

Body

I.   First word

II. Second word

III. Third word, etc.

Summary

Conclusion

Expository

Expository preaching is the traditional form for 'pulpiteers' for centuries. The word exposition is from the Latin, *'expositio'*, meaning to set forth, narration, or display. To set forth or explain the message of the biblical text. In expository preaching the sermon is designed to communicate what the text says, including its meaning for the contemporary audience.

The expository design is probably the most common design of preachers today. It is age-old, and often hailed as the only true form of biblical preaching. The expository design composes the message and develops the main points by using a block of Scripture that is expounded upon one verse at a time. (It's the familiar 'read on' in our urban pulpits.) The block of Scripture can be a chapter, a parable, or an account of a specific event.

In expository preaching you must first discover the text's intended theological meaning. This design is preferred because it engages the audience in following the Scriptures as they are read aloud. Some do not prefer it because it is limited in scope, isolating other parts of the Bible message. Some of the challenges with using the expository design are:

- Thoughts may become scattered
- Too much information
- Lose focused on the main point.

Introduction
Thematic Statement

Body
I. First verse — Read on!
II. Second verse
III. Third verse, etc.

Summary
Conclusion

Numerical

The numerical design may be used when you have a list of main points. It is similar to the categorical design, except it may or may not have large blocks of information. In fact, the flexibility of the numerical design is ideal for detailing a list of steps, causes or kinds. For example: *The three 'R's or the Seven attributes of Holiness; the 10 commandments, etc.*

The numerical design is often used combined with another design like topical or textual. It goes well with information that should be written down.

Introduction

Thematic Statement

Body

I. First verse

II. Second verse

III. Third verse, etc.

Summary

Conclusion

Sequential

The sequential design is like the numerical in that it involves a list of movements or steps, but in this design, they must have a natural sequence. For instance: The events leading to the return of the prodigal son; Salvation must be preached in sequence: repentance is before water baptism, etc.

Introduction

Thematic Statement

Body

I. First step

II. Second step

III. Third step, etc.

Summary

Conclusion

Spatial

The spatial design is similar to an illustrative sermon. It tells a story. In fact, the story is taken from the biblical narrative in the text. You've heard the expression, a picture is worth a thousand words. Stories are often more effective in conveying a message because they engage our imagination and emotions.

Introduction

Thematic Statement

Body

I. Opening scene

II. Mid scene

III. Closing scene

Summary

Conclusion

Textual

The textual design is much like expository and exegetical but smaller in content. It is more of a contextual design in that information is taken from the text and surrounding Scriptures. The book of Proverbs or Psalms may prove interesting to deliver from a textual design.

Introduction

Thematic Statement

Body

Scripture may contain points within the text.

Summary

Conclusion

Topical

This design is exactly what it says, 'a topic'. You select a topic and bring in supporting Scripture and illustrations. You may also include points, lists, sequences, etc.

Introduction

Thematic Statement

Body

I. First point

II. Second point

III. Third point, etc.

Summary

Conclusion

Contrast and Comparison

This complex design is used primarily with a revelation in mind. You literally expound on two situations from two different narratives. After you expound on each, you combine them and preach the contrast from the comparison. This is a very uncommon design. It takes a skillful speaker to be thorough, but not boring or unusually long in the delivery. It can be very colorful and informative if the Minister knows what to do. Otherwise, it can be awkward and confusing. It may even look like you've preached two messages and wasted a lot of time. Your points must come out in the combination of the two situations.

Introduction

Thematic Statement

Body

story + story = contrast

Summary

Conclusion

PREACHING ETIQUETTE

PUNCTUALITY - It is very important for a Minister to be punctual. Lateness shows a disrespect to the leadership, the people, and the meeting. The real problem with being constantly late is that it will cause you to become stressed and anxious, which will invariably effect the delivery of your message. Punctuality commands respect from your audience and increases confidence.

OPENING PRAYER - The opening prayer is always before the beginning of your message. Pray to bless the listener, the message, and the response (and sometimes yourself). Another approach is to give thanks for the presence of the Lord, the people, acknowledging Holy Spirit anointing, for the word of GOD to go forth unhindered. He/she is to take authority in the Spirit, to decree, and declare what will manifest in the service. The prayer should be brief (1-2 minutes).

CLOSING PRAYER - The closing prayer is done immediately after the message. This prayer is to seal the move of God that took place in the service, and to send the people home with a ben-a-diction (well-speaking). The minister may also include an altar call in the closing prayer, or a call to action by briefly reiterating the main theme of the message.

ALTAR CALLS – The altar call should be done immediately after the message, and should be an extension of the message. The most important altar call is always for salvation. When making an altar call for salvation or baptism, the Minister must be clear and concise, taking time and concern with biblical terminology. Remember, it is a sensitive and emotional time for anyone seeking God. Keep in mind that someone will always come to the altar, so be aware of the time. Calling for corporate prayer will always be an appropriate altar call. Prophesying is not always appropriate. Remember, *'The spirit of the prophet is subject to the prophet, so you can help it!'* (more in the chapter on the Altar Call).

OFFERING – How you present yourself in asking for an offering will often determine how people will respond in giving. Never make people feel uncomfortable in giving. NEVER miss an opportunity for them to sow into a particular need or blessing, but NEVER use manipulation. Some may need the inspiration of the Minister, because your words can activate their faith...but,

NEVER as a hustle. Remember, faith comes by hearing! Always pray a blessing over the Tithes and offerings. (Read more in the chapter on Tithes and Offerings)

DRESS - Ministers appearance should be a unique blend of modesty and sophistication. You have a responsibility to reflect the image of Christ. A female minister should never show a cleavage or wear a short, tight skirt to the pulpit, (or while ministering on the altar). Male and female ministers are to be well groomed, especially hair, teeth, and nails. What you wear does matter!

Homiletics

What questions do you ask when determining the purpose of your message?

    a.

    b.

    c.

2. What is the primary reason to search the Scriptures concerning your topic? What is the consequence of not finding a Scripture?

3. From what five places should you collect data?

    a.

    b.

    c.

    d.

    e.

4. Where should you select your main points?
   Should it be supported by Scripture?   Why?

5. What should be your primary focus?

6. What are three benefits of a design?

    a.

    b.

    c.

7. Why should you add illustrations?

8. When should you write an introduction? Why?

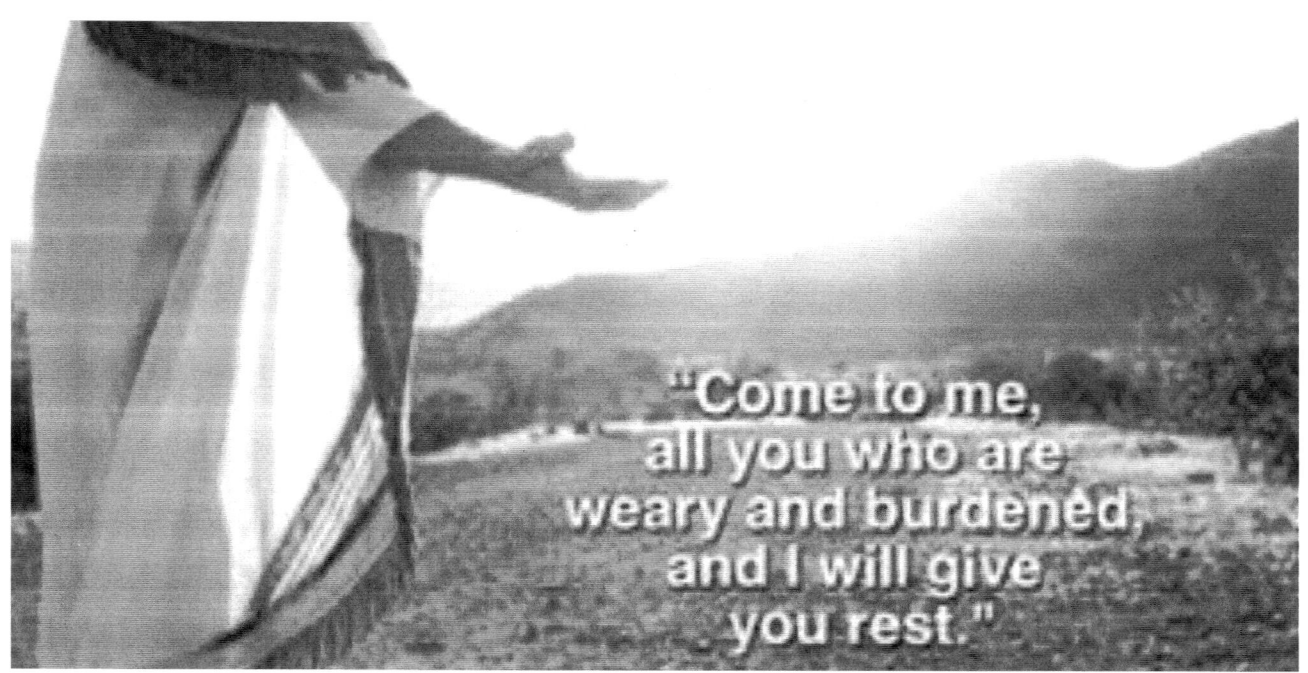
"Come to me, all you who are weary and burdened, and I will give you rest."

ALTAR CALL

HISTORY

OPPOSITION

PROCEDURE

'. . . And he went on his journey from the South as far as Bethel, to the place where his tent had been at the beginning, between Bethel and Ai, the place of the altar which he had made there at first. And there Abram called on the name of the LORD.' Gen. 13:3-4

THE ALTAR

Come unto me, all ye that labour and are heavy laden, and I will give you rest.
Matt. 11:28

The 'Altar Call' is an invitation to come to the altar in response to the preached Word of God. In most messages, a minister is speaking to give information or to move the hearers to a particular action. The altar call is often (but not always) given at the end of the message. Whether the sermon is persuasive or informative, the Divine intent is to prompt a 'heart felt' response. It is an invitation to engage the presence of GOD. The call to 'come forth' likely originated from the location of the altar (which was typically at the front of the pulpit). In the New Testament, especially with John the Baptist, many people **came forth** in response to his teachings and were baptized. The Bible records that Jesus preached messages without compromise and afterwards made the request, *"**Come** to Me, all you who labor and are heavy laden, and I will give you rest." (Matt. 11:38) "If any man thirst, let him **come** unto me, and drink." (Jn. 7:37)*

Apostle Paul preached *"**Repent**, therefore, and be converted, that your sins may be blotted out"* (Acts 3:19). *"**Be reconciled** unto God."* (2 Cor. 5:20) and *"testified both to the Jews, and also to the Greeks, **repentance** toward God, and faith toward our Lord Jesus Christ."* (Acts 20:21) And many were **'counted'** as having added to the church daily. How were they counted? The 'call to repentance' was an invitation to **come** to and receive **life** in Christ. The apostles did not hesitate to hold out Christ as Savior to all who listened to their message.

HISTORY

When an invitation to come to Christ was given, it would stand to reason that someone would provide a place to come, if only for an embrace, a confirmation, or encouragement. I believe that extending *an invitation to come,* would be the request to make after preaching salvation, healing, or deliverance. However, there are conflicting opinions about the use and the need for the altar call. Some believe the altar call to be embarrassing and unnecessary. We will compare both sides of the controversy but first, let's look at the history of the altar call.

The word 'altar' is first mentioned in Genesis 8:20, *'Then Noah built an altar to the LORD, and took of every clean animal and every clean bird, and offered burnt-offerings on the altar.'* The Hebrew word for 'altar' and the verb 'to slaughter' are both derived from the same root word. Altar and slaughter were terms used in connection with the ritual of sacrificing animals to God as a covering for sin. The Greek words for altar also point to sacrificing animals. *(Could it be that Paul in Rom. 12:1 was referring to this kind of altar?)* The Israelites were not the first, or only people to use the altar. It was widely known in the ancient Middle East. In Megiddo, Canaanite temples and altars have been excavated dating back to centuries before the Israelites appeared and they were always used for sacrificing to a deity.

So, how did we get to the altar call? Historically, many people consider Charles Grandison Finney (1792-1875) to be the "father" of the altar call. But, Finney did not begin giving public invitations until long after Methodists had made the altar call a regular part of their camp meetings. Finney, ordained as a Presbyterian minister in 1823, however, did more than anyone to establish altar calls as an accepted and widespread practice in America. The method was designed to force decisions and get results. And so it did, with slight variations. The new method spread with increasing popularity through Finney, and later Dwight L. Moody, R. A. Torrey, Billy Sunday, Bob Jones, Gipsy Smith, John R. Rice, Billy Graham and most of the 19th-20th century evangelicals. They all employed the altar call with great success.[1]

OPPOSITION

Even though the invitation system had success, there was also a dramatic backlash against the altar call, (which has been in use for about 200 years), claiming that it was not biblical or, in some cases, not ethical. In fact, for nearly 19 centuries no one had ever heard of the altar call. George Whitefield, Jonathan Edwards, and even John Wesley had never even heard of it. And Charles Spurgeon, although well acquainted with the practice, refused to adopt it and

---

[1] Walk the Aisle I Christian History - Christianity Today. (n.d.).

even criticized it. Some of the arguments for NOT using an altar call are listed here:

- The altar call requires a person to physically respond. The gospel call is for a man to run to **Christ**. But never to be confused with a command to move anywhere physically.
- Neither Jesus nor His apostles ever instructed anyone that in order to be saved they must "come to the front", or "come for prayer", or to a geographical location.
- The focus has shifted from the spiritual to the physical, from the internal to the external. People said, *'The meeting was "wonderful" because so many people "went forward."'*
- Some began to believe that they were saved by walking an aisle, correctly answering a series of questions, and then praying a prescribed prayer. Can walking an aisle contribute anything to a spiritual conversion?
- The altar call can promote false assurance. Some believed they were Christians because they were baptized as infants or as adults. The same way many people, who have "walked the aisle", believe that if they would "come forward" and "make a decision", they would be saved.
- It confuses profession of faith with saving faith. Conversion is not a confession or a decision.
- To some, the call to the front of the church is intrusive and embarrassing.

While these are valid assumptions, they are simply that… assumptions. We would have to assume that the use of the 'altar call' would give someone, (especially in these times) the impression that everyone who comes to the altar is actually converted. We would also have to assume that the person on the altar believes this as well. We may also consider that the apostles didn't have altar calls, (as we know them) but, they obviously had a vast number of people come forth at one time. (Example: 3000 were added to the Church in Acts 2:41.)

We believe the altar call is essential today because of the hands-on contact that people so desperately need. However, we should have another designated place for those who need counseling or special attention when they come to the altar. It is imperative that we consider the cultural/historical gap when we compare the New Testament church (including the early19th Century Church), with the familiar practice of the altar call that we see today. We must also realize that whenever we take a simple practice such as calling people forth, and make it an inflexible tradition, we step into intolerance and legalism. The congregations in the time of Christ were not standing in churches or conference centers, but on mountainsides and sea shores which would also require a 'different approach' to giving an invitation or making an 'altar call.'

PROCEDURE

The preached Word demands a response, and a Minister should always preach with that specific response in mind. The altar call should be planned or at least anticipated. It should never become simply something you do after you preach. How you make an altar call should be determined by the leading of the Holy Spirit, as well as, you after accessing your audience.

There are different reasons for extending an invitation, or making an altar call, such as:

- To **receive Jesus** Christ as Lord and Savior
- To **be baptized in water** or in the **Holy Spirit**
- To **join** the fellowship (explain how members are received)
- To **repent** of a specific sin
- To **return** to Christ (Backsliders)
- To request **prayer** for a personal need, baby baptisms,
- To respond to a **specific challenge** from the message (healing, breakthrough, deliverance, etc.)
- To **dedicate** babies or newborns

Typically, after the Word has been preached, the Minister will make the appeal for the altar call. Although you can never predict what might happen during this time, you should be prepared by doing the following:

1. Have an assistant help when praying for people (preferably another minister).

2. Be conscious of the time. Ask what has to be done after the altar call. In fact, it would be wise to find out if the meeting has made time in the program for an altar call. If you're in a church setting, the atmosphere in the service will determine the proper timing for the altar call.

3. Be sensitive to the request made by the person coming to the altar. Unfortunately, some people are not serious. They are simply addicted to having prayer or prophesies. You may also encounter people that are demonic plants, sent to distract you and cause a disturbance. Others need counseling and cannot be dealt with at the altar in the short amount of time. There should be someone to assist them with follow-up or an appointment with church leaders.

4. Your attire is very important. You do not want to wear revealing or tight fitting clothes, especially at the altar. You should never wear something that will open, rise, or gap in case someone falls or accidentally pull you down. Hygiene is also very important. You should always be conscious of body odor, bad breath, or loud perfumes. Never wear anything that would be distracting from the presence of God.

5. Although the altar call should be in response to the message and/or your appeal, you should never assume that everyone has come in response to your invitation. Always ask why they came up before you begin to pray for them.

6. Never allow other altar workers to touch the person while you're ministering unless you direct them. Every one has a vibration and one negative touch can break a spiritual connection. Untrained and unsuspecting altar workers have experienced negative or demonic transferences at the altar. (No fear intended) Many people think that it's a myth. But, I beg to differ. After many years and several personal experiences while working the altars, I've discovered that it's not a spiritual playground.

7. Be careful with the opposite sex. You should always request a male altar worker to help with men, and a female altar worker to help with women.

We are living in a time when God is unveiling His chosen. Miracles, signs and wonders will be commonplace. His sons and His daughters will prophesy, and He will SHOW… signs in the heavens and in the earth. Prayer will ALWAYS be your strength at the altar…and for ANY **work** of the ministry!

1.   What was the original use for the altar?

2.   Who made making an altar call popular?

3.   List 7 reasons to make an altar call.

   1.

   2.

   3.

   4.

   5.

   6.

   7.

4.   What should determine the reason for an altar call?

5.   Why is attire and hygiene important when working the altar?

6.   Should you assume that a person comes to the altar for the same reason you made the call?   Y/N   Why? or Why Not?

7.   Should you allow other altar works and ministers to touch the people that you're ministering to? Y/N   Why? or Why Not?

PRAYER

CORPORATE

PERSONAL

CEREMONIAL

*Praying always with all prayer and supplication in the Spirit, and watching
thereunto with all perseverance and supplication for all saints;*
Eph. 6:18

PRAYER

"And He spake a parable unto them to this end, that men ought always to pray, and not to faint." Luke 18:1

We were created by God — for God! We have been hard-wired for intimacy with God. We have a natural longing and a sense of emptiness that's designed to be filled by Him. However, because of 'Adamic amnesia,' we do not always realize that it is God that we desire. That spiritual craving and hunger that we feel are for Him. Blaise Pascal, a 17th Century Christian philosopher said, *"What else does this craving, and this helplessness, proclaim but that there was once in man a true happiness, of which all that now remains is the empty print and trace?"* Prayer is our Divine re-connect. Prayer is **NOT** Preaching! It is ignorant and carnal to pray to incite a response from the people. We pray to get a response from God. Prayer is Divine communication from the earth to His throne. It is a means of intimate communion with God. It is the medium by which we make the invisible visible. Prayer strengthens you against the powers of the world, the flesh, and the devil. Prayer will change things, situations, circumstances, and people. However, most of all, prayer will change YOU! A consistent prayer life is foundational for any authentic ministry.

THREE CATEGORIES OF PRAYER

CORPORATE PRAYER - Also called a solemn assembly, corporate prayer is where people come together to pray for a particular reason, or at the same time. Corporate intercessory prayer is one of the most powerful weapons in the life of a Believer. Corporate prayer creates an atmosphere for the presence of God. Corporate Unity is a bi-product of corporate prayer. You can move mountains with the power of unity in prayer. Everyone is spiritually strengthened! God never intended for His people to be islands, but a massive Body moving in synergistic, choreographic unity with Holy Spirit! If two or more come together in His Name, He is there!

"If I shut up the heavens so there is no rain, or if I command the locust to devour the land, or if I send pestilence among My people, and My people who are called by My Name humble themselves and pray, and seek My face, and turn from their wicked ways, then I will hear from heaven, will forgive their sin, and will heal their land." 2 Chr. 7:13-14

Believers were in corporate prayer in the Upper Room. (Acts 2:1) Jehoshaphat called the people together to seek the Lord in corporate prayer. (2 Chr. 20:4) Believers were praying for Peter in corporate prayer. (Acts12:12) Corporate prayer creates an atmosphere for miracles, healing, deliverance, and prophetic ministry.

PERSONAL PRAYER - Your personal prayer time is when you're alone with God. In these special periods of personal communion, you give yourself, and all that concerns you, to God. The secret of spiritual transformation is when you connect in prayer with Holy Spirit and receive a Divine download. In prayer you learn to discern the voice of God, which is crucial for spiritual stamina and focus. When you establish a regular time of prayer, the Lord begins to tug on your spirit at *that exact time* each night (or day). He takes pleasure in communing with His people. A minister should study Scriptures especially for their prayers, always praying the Word of God. Personal prayer doesn't mean selfish prayer. It's a time when you're more like Christ than ever... expressing unadulterated love for Him, His Will, His Word, and His people— ALL for His Glory! You will never mature spiritually or advance in ministry with a deficient, inconsistent prayer life.

CEREMONIAL PRAYER - Prayers for specific events such as weddings, meetings, political events, dinners, or programs are called formal or ceremonial prayers. These prayers should only address that which is relevant to the occasion or event. Ceremonial prayers should not be lengthy (1 or 2 minutes). The formal prayer should focus on acknowledging and beseeching God. The audience may be asked to stand or bow their heads before the prayer begins. The minister should exit the platform after the prayer. It is rude for a minister to take advantage and speak to an audience for any reason other than to pray, unless the coordinator has given prior permission.

KINDS OF PRAYER

PRAISE/WORSHIP — To celebrate GOD's power, love, and Worth. Psa. 100:1-4
INTERCESSION — To entreat God on behalf of someone else. Rom. 8:27
PETITION — To ask for something with importunity. Luke 18:1
SUPPLICATION — To entreat for, or request. Phil. 4:6
FORGIVENESS — To request or seek mercy and forgiveness. Matt. 6:14
PROPHETIC / TONGUES — To pray in the Spirit. 1 Cor. 14:14

Prayer

OUR FATHER - Relationship

WHO ART IN HEAVEN - Praise

HOLY IS THY NAME -   Nature and Character

THY KINGDOM COME, THY WILL BE DONE ON EARTH AS IN HEAVEN -

Intercession

GIVE ME THIS DAY - Petition

FORGIVE ME MY DEBTS (TRESPASSES) - Repentance, Mercy

AS I FORGIVE DEBTORS (TRESPASSERS) - Forgiveness

LEAD ME NOT INTO TEMPTATION   - Supplication

DELIVER ME FROM EVIL - Protection

THINE IS THE KINGDOM, POWER, AND I GIVE YOU THE GLORY -

Worship

FASTING

BIBLICAL FAST

FASTING BASICS

WHY YOU SHOULD FAST

'Is this not the fast that I have chosen: To loose the bonds of wickedness, To undo the heavy burdens, To let the oppressed go free, And that you break every yoke?'

Isa. 58:6

BIBLICAL FASTING

'Is it a fast that I have chosen, A day for a man to afflict his soul? Is it to bow down his head like a bulrush, And to spread out sackcloth and ashes? Would you call this a fast, And an acceptable day to the LORD? Isa. 58:7

Fasting is abstaining from food. The Hebrew word for fast is *'tsoom'* which means 'to cover the mouth.' It means to omit meals for a set period of time. Early Christians have normally associated fasting with repentance and cleansing. However, the benefits of fasting are both spiritual and natural. Fasting is a powerful weapon that declares spiritual war on the world, flesh, and the devil! But, it also gives the digestive system a rest as it cleanses the body of toxins.

We believe that all ministers should practice fasting. Fasting does not draw GOD closer to you— fasting will bring you closer to GOD. It opens your spirit to become more sensitive to the leading of Holy Spirit. Fasting intensifies your time of prayer and study. Fasting and prayer develops discipline and self-control. When you lead a fasted and consecrated lifestyle, nothing will be impossible for you in the realm of the Spirit. When you fast, you can **expect** GOD to reveal Himself. Fasting destroys spiritual bondages and breaks carnal yokes. Jesus fasted 40 days and nights. Moses fasted, Esther fasted, David fasted, Paul fasted, and WE fast to the Glory of GOD. There are many more instances recorded in the Bible where believers used the power of fasting listed below.

Fasting was observed on occasions of public calamities, 2 Sam. 1:12; Afflictions, Psa. 35:13; approaching danger, Esther 4:16; Ordination of ministers, Acts 13:3; 14:23. Accompanied by prayer, Dan. 9:3; Confession of sin, 1 Sam. 7:6; Neh. 9:1, 2; humiliation, Deut. 9:18; Neh. 9:1; reading of the Scriptures, Jer. 36:6. Habitual: by John's disciples, Matt. 9:14; by Anna, Luke 2:37; by Cornelius, Acts 10:30; by Paul, 2 Cor. 6:5; 11:27. Prolonged: for three weeks, by Daniel, Dan. 10:2, 3; forty days, by Moses, Ex. 24:18; 34:28; Deut. 9:9, 18; Elijah, 1 Kin. 19:8; Jesus, Matt. 4:2; Mark 1:12, 13; Luke 4:1, 2; By Paul, at the time of his conversion, Acts 9:9. Of the disciples, at the time of the consecration of Barnabas and Saul, Acts 13:2, 3. Of the consecration of the elders, Acts 14:23.[1]

---

[1]Swanson, J., & Nave, O. (1994). *New Nave's Topical Bible*. Oak Harbor

PERSONAL FAST

Pastor Jentezen Franklin is my model when it comes to fasting! Below you will find the listing for his fasting guide. I usually fast for 21 days each year in January. I developed this particular method for my personal fast many years ago. For each week of the 21 days, I alternate as I increase food intake. Week one (usually while consecrating in our Sanctuary) is lemon water and distilled water only (The Master Cleanse). Week two are juices and water. Week three, vegetable broth, juices, and water. Because there are so many ways to fast, I should remind you that it is personal. You should do what works for you.

Fasting Basics by Jentezen Franklin

Simply stated, biblical fasting is refraining from food for a spiritual purpose. According to the Bible, there are three duties of every Christian: give, pray and fast. Biblical fasting takes a lot of discipline and strength—strength which you can only receive from God. Your private discipline will bring you rewards in Heaven, says Matthew 6. When you give God your first through fasting, prayer and giving at the beginning of the year, you set the course for the entire year.[1]

Why should I fast?
1 Are you in need of healing or a miracle?
2 Do you need the tender touch of God in your life?
3 Is there a dream inside you that only He can make possible?
4 Are you in need of a fresh encounter?
5 Do you desire a deeper, more intimate, powerful relationship with the Lord?
6 Are you ready to have heightened sensitivity to the desires of God?
7 Do you need to break from bondages that have been holding you hostage?
8 Is there a friend or loved one that needs Salvation?
9 Do you desire to know God's will for your life?

BIBLICAL FASTING FOCUS
MATTHEW 6:33 "But seek ye first the kingdom of God, and his righteousness; and all these things shall be added unto you."

---

[1]Jentezen Franklin <https://www.jentezenfranklin.org/fasting/>

We want to encourage you to target your prayers during the fast (e.g., deliverance, healing, schools, leaders, etc,). The Bible instructs us to continually pray for our leaders (1 Tim. 2:1-2). When we lift up our leaders, here in the United States and around the world, we can expect God's peace in our lives and in our nation.

Another great promise, from the book of Isaiah, proclaims that the chosen fast will "undo the heavy burdens and let the oppressed go free." We are living in tough economic times and we know that so many people are under a financial burden. As we come together to fast and pray, we believe that your burdens will be lifted and that ideas for financial blessings will be released into your life!
We encourage you to seek the Lord in prayer and let your decisions about your biblical fasting come from Him. Ask the Lord to show you areas to target during your time of fasting and prayer. We believe that, as we pray and seek God and give Him our best at the first of the year, He will bless our ENTIRE year!

For a free copy of the fasting guide https://www.jentezenfranklin.org/fasting
Or go online and download the Daniel Fast.

WHY FAST:

- **To draw closer to GOD** - *Joel 2:12- Therefore also now, saith the LORD, turn ye even to me with all your heart, and with <u>fasting</u>, and with weeping, mourning.*

- **To receive revelation** – *Dan. 9:3- And I set my face unto the LORD GOD, to seek by prayer and supplications, with <u>fasting</u>.*

- **To receive direction**- *Acts 13:2,3- As they ministered to the LORD, and fasted, the Holy Ghost said, separate me Barnabas and Saul for the work whereunto I have called them. And when they had fasted and prayed, they laid their hands on them and sent them away.*

- **For answers to prayer** – *2 Sam. 12:16- David therefore besought GOD for the child and David fasted, and went in and lay all night upon the earth.*

- **To overcome temptation**- *Matt. 4:1,2- Then was Jesus led up of the spirit into the wilderness to be tempted of the devil. And when He had fasted 40 days and nights, he afterwards was hungry.*

- **To break the power of sin and the devil** - *Matt. 17:21- Howbeit, this kind goes not out but by prayer and fasting.*

PROPHETIC MINISTRY

WHAT IS PROPHECY

WHO CAN PROPHESY

THE THREE VOICES

'For no prophecy was ever produced by the will of man, but men spoke from God as they were carried along by the Holy Spirit.' 2 Pet. 1:21 (NLV)

PROPHETIC MINISTRY

'For the Lord GOD does nothing without revealing his secret to his servants the prophets.'
Amos 3:7

The Spirit of God is sending a clarion call to prophets, and Believers everywhere, to prepare for the natural and spiritual challenges that lie ahead. The Glory of God is about to be revealed like never before! The Scriptures, known as the Olivet discourse, are key to understanding the spiritual condition of our society and the world at large. One only has to look around and see that Matthew 24-25 are the headlines in our daily news. Jesus spoke specifically and emphatically about the spirit of deception in Matt. 24:4-5 which says, *'take heed that no man deceives you. For many shall come in my name, saying, I am Christ (the Anointed Sent One) and shall deceive many.'* (Amp) We are warned about deception 3 times in Matt. 24, and many times throughout Scripture. Many will claim that they come in the Name of the Lord with a word, a dream, or a vision, and will deceive many. Spiritual deception is already evident with the increase of distorted bible teachings, doctrines of devils, and demonic occult manifestations. The Apostle Paul gives a pointed warning about deception in his letter to Timothy,

'...having a form of godliness but denying its power. And from such people turn away!"For the time is coming when people will not endure sound teaching, but having itching ears, they will accumulate for themselves teachers to suit their passions, and will turn away from listening to the truth and wander off into myths.' *2 Tim. 3:3-4 (NKJV)*

Be Not deceived! We must be sensitive to the **Voice of GOD** like never before. But, listen. Although these are the worst of times, they're also the best of times. We are compassed about with great darkness. But, we're also living in one of the most prophetic and Spiritually heightened times in history. It is a time when GOD has released an army of Believers that will establish His Kingdom, infiltrate governments, subdue nations, bring healing, deliverance, and Glory to His Name. All under the auspices of His Spirit and the power of 'His' Word! GOD is releasing a prophetic utterance that will strategically place and position His army for conquest and victory called the 'Mysteries of the Kingdom.' The Greek word for mystery is **'musterion.'** This word means: *'a series of truths that were given* *to someone who was initiated into a secret society; a secret that was only reveal in part to a select few, and a military term for battle plans that only the general and his sons knew.'* Well, we are about to receive battle plans and mission instructions from our General for this end time campaign! **We are also about to revisit the purpose and the power of prophetic ministry.**

'...And on my servants and on my handmaidens I will pour out in those days of my Spirit; **and they shall prophesy: And I will show** *wonders in heaven above, and signs in the earth beneath...' Acts 2:17-18 (KJV)*

Prophecy is the language of GOD. It is released by GOD to assist us in building the BODY of Christ and establishing His Kingdom on the earth.

In his 'Jumpstart Prophetic Activation Manual,' Dr. G.E. Bradshaw defines the prophetic anointing: *'It is the vehicle for manifestation of God's voice, will, purpose and intentions through believers. It may work through any of the five spiritual senses which are a parallel of the five natural senses.'*[1]

Dr. Bruce Cook has written an in-depth study on prophecy and the prophetic in his book 'Partnering with the Prophetic.' In it, he calls attention to the deceptive lure of the Church:

'In an age where prime time television programming includes The Medium to showcase the abilities of psychics, and series on zombies, werewolves, and vampire slayers, plus millions more being attracted to New Age theology, it's time to receive, utilize and honor prophecy and prophets in the church as God intended, so that the church stops calling the psychic hotlines and spending billions of dollars a year asking the world for answers that God has already given to His prophets.[2]

Dr. Cook expounds on, and exposes the multidimensional practices and manifestations of prophetic ministry. 'Partnering with the Prophetic,' is a comprehensive work on prophetic portfolios, protocols, patterns and processes.

Prophecy **is GOD speaking His mind, will, plans, purposes, thoughts, and intentions** to, and through, His people for the building of His Kingdom. We shouldn't be running from the prophetic, but to it! GOD is unveiling and raising authentic prophets, who understand submission to spiritual authority and the responsibilities that comes with the gift. While prophetic ministry has a lot to do

---

[1]Bradshaw, Dr. Gordon, (2010) 'Prophetic Jumpstart' pg 9

[2]Cook, Bruce, Dr. (2014-02-01). Partnering With The Prophetic: Portfolios, Protocols, Patterns & Processes

with your natural abilities, the prophet is a speaker **for** GOD. Although you must develop your own prophetic style (whether seer, hearing, visions, dreams, etc.), your words are not the production of your own spirit, but from the mouth of GOD.

'For no prophecy was ever produced by the will of man, but men spoke from God as they were carried along by the Holy Spirit.' 2 Pet. 1:21(NLV)

Prophecy is the supreme exercise in **surrendering** to the awesome unction of Holy Spirit. Consequently, in all humility, I believe that it is also one of the most abused, misused and mistaken manifestation of Holy Spirit operating in the Body of Christ today. When you encounter the many people that have been **wounded, confused, and misguided** by those who are **unharnessed, unlearned, and perverting the prophetic,** you will definitely see the need for a Divine warning, and instructions, concerning prophesying and prophetic ministry.

'Thus saith the LORD of hosts, Hearken not unto the words of the prophets that prophesy unto you: they make you vain: they speak a vision of their own heart, and not out of the mouth of the LORD.'   Jer. 23:16 (KJV)

In my book 'Yielding to the Power of the Prophetic,'[1] you will find instructions and information that will sharpen your sensitivity and your spiritual ear. You will get a better understanding of how prophecy is used for edification, encouragement, and comfort. (1 Cor. 14:3) You will be introduced to three (of many) prophetic voices and be able to discern the differences. You will study the power of prayer and faith in prophetic ministry. You will learn how to recognize false prophets and the carnal tactics and practices of presumptuous, untrained people, who become instruments of deception for the Body of Christ. The Bible says in Ezekiel 13:2,

'Son of man, prophesy against the prophets of Israel that prophesy, and say thou unto them that prophesy out of their own hearts, Hear ye the word of the LORD.'

Dr. Bill Hamon in his book, 'God's Prophetic Voice Today'[2] wrote,

'I believe that this is an age in which God is raising up a multitude of prophets who are anointed and appointed— honest, true, trained, and experientially

---

[1] Powell, Dr. Glories (2016-01-01). 'Yielding to the Power of the Prophetic'

[2] Hamon, Bill; Roberts, Oral (2011-07-28). Prophets and Personal Prophecy: God's Prophetic Voice Today (p. 35). Destiny Image.

matured. But mixed in among these will be found those prophets who are ignorant, immature, and even false. There will be no place to hide the saints from them in this day of mass media reaching into every home. So the only true salvation from the enemy's falsehoods will be to expose the saints purposefully and properly to true prophets, educate them to discern true from false, and train them in how to respond.'

These, and other powerful men and women of God, are saying in concert that there will be a time of unveiling, but there will also be a time of separating the true from the false. Since prophecy is a vocal gift, it deals primarily with speaking and hearing the Voice of God. Unfortunately, there are many other voices that can be equally persuasive if you're unable to discern the difference. In the next three paragraphs, we will look at the three most impacting voices in the life of the Believer—the voice of God, the voice of Satan, and the voice of man.

THE VOICE OF GOD

"My sheep hear my voice, and I know them, and they follow me." (John 10:27)
A common question in Christian circles is, *'How do I know if it was God speaking to me?'* Knowing the voice of God is foundational to following and obeying God. It is vitally important for every believer to be able to recognize the voice of God in the midst of the noisy conglomeration of voices in our minds. The mind is much like a radio where sound travels on frequencies. Each voice of relevance in your life has its own frequency. The Spirit of God is the frequency for the voice of God, but you must be tuned in. This frequency was created after the ascension of Christ according to John 14:26, *'But the Comforter, which is the Holy Ghost, whom the Father will send in my name, he shall teach you all things, and bring all things to your remembrance, whatsoever I have said unto you.'*

'Now we have received, not the spirit of the world, but the spirit which is of God; that we might know the things that are freely given to us of God.' 1 Cor. 2:12

The Holy Spirit was sent to be the Voice of God to man.

God speaks to us, **by** His Spirit **to** our spirit. When you begin to hear God's voice through your spirit, it sounds a lot like your voice. We learn to discern God's voice from our inner voice through prayer and training from Holy Spirit.

*'Which things also we speak, not in the words which man's wisdom teaches, but which the Holy Ghost **teaches**; comparing spiritual things with spiritual.'*
1 Cor. 2:13

It takes time to learn to discern the voice of God. God will speak something simple and relevant to His word. There may be a certain emotion or feeling, (i.e., peace, anger, power, etc.) associated with the Words you hear. By faith you believe it's the voice of God. As you begin to build on each experience, your faith will become strong enough to recognize and operate freely by a prophetic unction. God will give you confirmation and instruction from other prophetic people as well.

FAITH AND SCRIPTURE IN THE PROPHETIC

We are given prophecy to assist us in obtaining the mind of Christ. Dr. Bruce Cook clearly explains the importance of faith and the Word of God saying, *'Prophecy is a gift, a tool, and a weapon, but it is not a drug, and it is not a substitute for faith; however, it is designed and intended to enhance and strengthen faith in the believer. Prophecy is also intended to complement a knowledge of Scripture and personal spiritual maturity and character development, not replace them.'*[1]

Faith is the ability to believe God for 'anything.' Faith is the foundation of the prophetic. **Your faith matures and increases as the prophetic anointing develops in your life**. Romans 12:6 instructs us to prophesy according to the measure of faith. Romans 10:17 says, *'For faith …. by hearing, and hearing God!'* Those who hear God, having their senses exercised to know God's voice, will speak with authority and conviction, not double-minded or resorting to verbal gymnastics. The true prophet, yielding to the power of prophecy, in faith, will see powerful results. *'…And on my servants and on my handmaidens I will pour out in those days of my Spirit; and **they shall prophesy And I will show,** wonders in heaven above, and signs in the earth beneath.'* Acts 2:17-18

*'Howbeit when He, the Spirit of truth, is come, …he will show you things to come. He shall glorify me, for he shall receive of mine, and **shall show it unto you.'**
John 16:13*

---

[1]Cook, Bruce, Dr. (2014-02-01). Partnering With The Prophetic: Portfolios, Protocols, Patterns & Processes (Kindle Locations 959-961).

The Word of God is forever settled in heaven. God will never give you a prophecy that contradicts Scripture. It is therefore, vital that a minister be well versed in Scripture. The Word of God is good for rebuke, correction, doctrine, and instruction in righteousness. (2 Tim. 3:16) Prophecy is given for warning, judgement, edification, encouragement, and comfort (1 Cor. 14: 31). Notice how **the Word of God (logos)** is very similar to **the Utterance of God (rhema)**. Knowledge of the Scriptures is foundational to prophetic accuracy.

THE VOICE OF SATAN

'But I am afraid that just as Eve was deceived by the serpent's cunning, your minds may somehow be led astray from your sincere and pure devotion to Christ.' 2 Cor. 11:3

Recognizing the voice of Satan is much like recognizing the voice of God. This demonic voice also has a certain sound and a certain frequency, but not the frequency of the Holy Spirit. **He cannot speak through your human spirit**, but he can speak to your mind. To fully understand how to recognize Satan's voice is to understand deception. Satan will try to imitate your inner voice, and plant suggestions into your mind. The best way to guard against deceptive, demonic thoughts is to monitor and guard your thinking. The Bible tells us in 1 Peter 5:8 *'Be sober, be vigilant; because your adversary the devil as a roaring lion walks about seeking whom he may devour.'* The NLB says, *'Be serious and alert!'* You have an enemy that will do anything to divert you from your divine purpose.

Satan will attempt to speak with the same prophetic authority as God. Jesus said, *'My sheep **know** My voice and they follow Me.' John 10:27* But, this does not stop the enemy from attacking with his deceptive strategies. Satan is motivated by one purpose… to kill, steal and destroy your FAITH! He doesn't want your car, your money, or your position in the church…he wants your FAITH! He knows that without faith you cannot successfully operate in the prophetic. Without faith you can't stand on God's word. Without faith you cannot please God.

Satan cannot use his 'voice' to create on the earth realm. Satan can only entice you to speak his deceptive plans into existence. The enemy will also use others to speak lies to you through prophecy. A prime example is Matt. 8: 21-23, *"From that time Jesus began to show to His disciples that He must go to Jerusalem, and suffer many things from the elders and chief priests and scribes, and be killed, and be* raised the third day. Then Peter took Him aside and began to rebuke Him, saying, 'Far be it from You, Lord; this shall not happen to You!' But He turned and said to Peter, "Get behind Me, Satan! You are an offense to Me, for you are not mindful of the things of God, but the things of men." Jesus rebuked Peter because he allowed the enemy to speak into His destiny. Satan's voice contradicted the voice, mind, plans, purposes, will, and intentions of God. Listed below are three ways the voice of Satan can destroy purpose in the life of a believer through lies and deception.

1. **Satan speaks to your mind to create fear** - Not 'every' thought that comes to your mind is yours. The enemy is a master at mental manipulation. His favorite tactic is fear. He spews threats and fearful thoughts into your mind to cause you to doubt God's voice, and become terrified about your situation and your future. Fear will paralyze your faith. Fear will plant discouragement and depression. You must cast down imaginations that have been planted by the enemy. And bring every thought into captivity. (1 Cor. 10:4)

2. **Satan speaks through others to mislead with 'so called' prophecies** - People have been misled and deceived by receiving demonically inspired words given as prophecy. False prophets are instruments for demonic voices. They prophesy for unjust gain, by divination, false visions, and lies. The Lord warns of false prophets who may appear harmless and unidentifiable in sheep's wool. Even though every 'false prophet' is deadly and spiritually damaging, those who prophesy falsely through a lack of training or anointing are more dangerous, because the enemy can easily gain entrance through their naivety and ignorance.

3. **Satan speaks lies through divination, a spirit of deception** - This form of prophetic deception will be prevalent in the last days. 'But false prophets also arose among the people, just as there will be false teachers among you, who will secretly bring in destructive heresies, even denying the Master who bought them, bringing upon themselves swift destruction.' (2 Pet. 2:1) ESV The Bible says that many will turn away from sound doctrine and be overtaken with a spirit of rebellion. Many will do what is right in their own eyes. This demonic voice will create a renegade mentality, lacking accountability. It is a tool in the enemy's hand to infect the Body of Christ with confusion and disrespect for spiritual authority and leadership. Beware of the voice of Satan; it will always be in direct contradiction to God's Word.

THE VOICE OF MAN

Man's voice is more complicated to discern because man can speak and hear a verbal stream of words, as well as, an internal monolog called the 'inner voice.' But, whether it is hearing, speaking, or an internal monolog, all are processed by the cognitive (thought) process. The inner monolog is happening within the human mind at all times. Your internal voice speaks to your mind in day-to-day operations deciphering and analyzing actions and activities around you. You talk to yourself constantly. The problem with your 'inner voice' is that you can't always discern whether it's your voice. It could be your voice, God's voice, or Satan's voice. So, it is imperative that you are able to discern the difference between voices. Ultimately, God's thoughts should be your thoughts.

God speaks a word of knowledge, a word of wisdom, or makes an impression on your spirit, but that impression must still go through your cognitive process. Divine revelation, instructions, and guidance enters your mind through the medium of thought. It is the Holy Spirit speaking **to you**. But, prophecy is not a word of knowledge, or a word of wisdom, doctrine, or revelation (although they may be used during a prophetic delivery). Prophecy is God speaking **through** you! God's voice transcends your thinking, as it flows to you on a higher spiritual frequency. It's called a Divine Utterance. This utterance has its own frequency and dimension. *True* **prophecy does not flow from a thought process**. God speaking through you (often using your mind, will, and emotions) is very powerful. The problem is that we have grouped 'divinely inspired' words of instruction, warning, edification, wisdom, and comfort all together under the heading of 'prophecy' (which is not Scriptural). **Everyone that prophesies is not a prophet. Neither is every inspired word a prophecy.** You partner with God in a prophetic utterance only in the fact that you yield yourself to Holy Spirit as a divine conduit. The Hebrew word **'nabi'** meaning 'bubbling forth,' clearly depicts the act of God's word bubbling up through your spirit in a verbal flow. Only a true prophet will understand the undeniable power of this revelatory gift.

When you study 1 Cor. 14:3, you will find, through contextual analysis, that the subject of prophecy is comparative and not superlative. Paul is comparing prophecy with tongues. He is not suggesting that everyone can prophesy, but that prophesying is more effective for converting the unbeliever, and speaking in tongues (as was desired by the Corinthians) was only beneficial for the individual (unless it was interpreted). There is much to learn about the many nuances of prophecy and the prophetic—and there are many anointed writers on the subject.

The Prophetic

1. Define prophecy.

2. Why does GOD speak through people?

3. Why is Scripture important for prophetic ministry?

4. What is the importance of being submitted under a prophetic covering?

5. What are the benefits of writing down or recording the prophecies that you give or receive?

6. Why is it more difficult to discern the voice of man?

7. How can you recognize the voice of God, of Satan, and man?

8. How should you response to a novice perverting prophecy?

9. What are three deceptive ways that Satan speaks to destroy your purpose?

10. Who can prophesy?

11. Is there a difference between Word of Knowledge, Word of Wisdom, and Prophecy? Define each.

12. What is the difference between comparative and superlative? (see 1 Cor 14:3)

BAPTISM (Water)

THE MEANING OF BAPTISM

THE BAPTISMAL CEREMONY

INFANT BAPTISM

Then Peter said unto them, 'Repent, and be baptized every one of you in the name of Jesus Christ for the remission of sins, and ye shall receive the gift of the Holy Ghost.' Acts 2:38

THE BAPTISM

'For as many of you as were baptized into Christ have put on Christ.' Gal. 3:27

Water baptism was implemented since the first century. It was performed when someone submitted to a particular teaching and/or teacher. Baptisms were not exclusive to John the Baptist or the disciples of Jesus. The Pharisees and the Sadducees had baptisms. The Herodians had baptisms. So did Plato, Aristotle, and Socrates who were master teachers with students as disciples. To be baptized meant that you became a submitted follower of a master teacher. You came under his authority and became one with his philosophy. We are baptized in the Name (nature, character, and teachings) of Christ Jesus. It is our proclamation of becoming a follower of Yeshua. The word *'baptize'* is a transliteration of the Greek word *'baptizo.'* In turn, baptizo comes from the root word *bapto,* a term used in the first century for immersing a garment first into bleach, then into dye, ***both cleansing and changing the color of the cloth.***[1]

A baptized believer is one who has "put on Christ." Christ now claims you and instructs you. To be baptized in the Name of Jesus is to receive a new identity. Baptism celebrates becoming that new person. It is an outward demonstration of an inward cleansing. As stated in the tenets of our Faith, *'We believe in water baptism by immersion, in the name of the Lord Jesus Christ, therefore fulfilling the command of Christ.'* (Matt. 28:19; Acts 2:34-39, 10:47-48; Luke 24:37)

True repentance is essential to a changed life. Baptism without true repentance is simply getting wet. However, when a believer has accepted the finished work of Christ on the cross and has received the teachings of Christ according to Romans 10:9,10 only then are they eligible to receive the baptism in the Name of Jesus for the remission of sins, thereby being engrafted into the Body of Christ.

Rom. 6:3-5 *'Know ye not, that so many of us as were baptized into Jesus Christ were baptized into his death? 4) Therefore we are buried with him by baptism into death: that like as Christ was raised up from the dead by the glory of the Father, even so we also should walk in newness of life. 5) for if we have been planted together in the likeness of his death, we shall be also in the likeness of his resurrection:'*

---

[1]What is Baptism? - Clarifying Christianity. (n.d.). Retrieved from http://clarifyingchristianity.com/get_wet.shtml

The ordinance of baptism has been observed since the time of the OT patriarchs. It was originally referred to as the 'washings, ritual cleansing, purification, and in the New Testament church, it was called baptism of repentance.' Many have misunderstood the Scripture which reads:

'...in the days of Noah, while the ark was preparing, in which few... were saved by water; the like figure unto which even baptism doth also now save us (not the putting away of the filth of the flesh, but the answer of a good conscience toward God), by the resurrection of Jesus Christ who is gone into heaven.' (1 Pet. 3:18)

Salvation is by true repentance and faith in the LORD Jesus Christ, thereby receiving **the cleansing that can only come through the Blood of Jesus.** However, baptism is essential to salvation in that it was commanded by Jesus Christ who gave us the example by being baptized himself.

Before he ascended into heaven, Jesus said, "Go ye therefore, and teach all nations, baptizing them **in the name** of the Father, and of the Son, and of the Holy Ghost: teaching them to observe all things whatsoever I have commanded you: and, lo, I am with you always, even unto the end of the world." (Matt. 28:19) The Apostle Peter gave more clarity to this command and demonstrated it in the book of Acts. Peter answers the question **'What is the Name?'**

'Then Peter said unto them, Repent, and be baptized every one of you **in the name of Jesus Christ** for the remission of sins, and ye shall receive the gift of the Holy Ghost...Then they **that gladly received his word were baptized**: and the same day there were added unto them about three thousand souls.' Acts 2:38

We baptize in obedience to that command that today. **It represents the death, burial, and resurrection of Jesus Christ.** Before a person becomes a Believer, he/she is dead in sin. When a person is dead, they are buried. The water represents a grave. As a person is lowered into the water it symbolizes that they are being buried. The person being lifted up out of the water symbolizes being raised to walk in newness of Kingdom life, and dead to sin! Baptism then, is an outward show of an inward change. You no longer walk after the dictates of your flesh, but you now walk submitted to the dictates of the Covenant of God. The blood is applied and the Holy Spirit of God is given as a result of true conversion.

THE BAPTISMAL CEREMONY

Ministers should wear appropriate attire whenever performing water baptisms. (The officiating Minister traditionally wears a black or white baptismal robe or smock.) The assisting ministers need not wear smocks or robes, but should be appropriately dressed. (Colors and clothing may vary.) The minister should also wear a plastic material to stand in the baptismal pool. The assisting Minister meets with the candidates for baptism *(before the ceremony)* to answer any questions they may have so that the candidates fully understand what water baptism entails. The candidates will need a baptismal cap, gown and towels (which may be provided by the church).

The officiating Minister will say a prayer and read Scripture pertaining to water baptism. *(Matt. 28:19; Acts 2:38; Rom. 6:12; Acts 19)* Afterwards, he/she will give a brief (15 minutes) exhortation on the power and meaning of Baptism. (One of the assisting ministers may be assigned to read the Scripture and pray.) The candidates are escorted to the baptismal pool. The minister will then announce the names of the candidates. The candidate will stand at the front of the baptismal pool clothed and ready. The baptizing minister will extend his hand and receive her/him, turning the candidate in front of him and stop. The officiating Minister will then says to the candidate:

(First name of candidate), Do you believe that Jesus Christ died for your sins? Do you believe that you are being baptized into Christ?
I want you to repeat after me...
(The minister then recites each line of the following pledge with the candidate repeating each line, like a wedding vow.)
I believe that Christ Jesus died and was buried for my sins, and that He rose from the dead on the 3rd day in newness of life. I believe that I too, will be raised in newness of life in Jesus Name.
The minister says:
(Name of candidate), in obedience to the command of Christ and upon your public profession of faith, I baptize you in the name of the Lord Jesus Christ for the remission of sins. (Some ministries add *'in the name of the Father, Son, and Holy Spirit'*)

The minister then lifts the cupped hands of the candidate so he/she can grip his/her nose. The minister lowers him/her into the water, then raises him/her out again. (Before the service the minister should instruct the candidate to bend his/her knees as he/she is lowered into the water.)

The congregation will give an applause and begin to celebrate with the candidate with singing and praising God.

The candidate turns and leaves the baptismal pool. The minister closes the baptismal service in prayer.

After the ceremony the candidates will be presented with a Certificate of Baptism before the Congregation.

INFANT / CHILDREN BAPTISM

We believe that baptism is for those who have a full understanding of the consciousness of sin. Children are only dedicated to the LORD (and not water baptized) until they reach the age of accountability, and with the consent of the parent. The parents are instructed on the meaning of the Dedication Ceremony, and of the vows they are to make before GOD.
(We require that at least one of the parents be a member of the Church.)

The parents/guardian will stand before the congregation with the child. The officiating Minister will read the Biblical requirements and responsibility for raising a child in the admonition of the LORD. *Ephesians 6:4*
The Minister will anoint the child with oil and water while praying the **prayer of dedication**. The Parents will lay hands on the child and recite these vows.

- *We promise to raise our child in the knowledge and admonition of the LORD.*

- *We promise to provide for, protect, to nurture, and to train up our child according to the Word of GOD.*

- **We dedicate the life of our child to the will of GOD all the days of his/her life. In the Name of JESUS.**

The Officiating Minister will then present the parents/guardian with a Certificate of Dedication.

COMMUNION

UNDERSTANDING THE LORD'S SUPPER

COMMUNION CEREMONY

'Take, eat: this is my body, which is broken for you: this do in remembrance of me. After the same manner also he took the cup, when he had supped, saying, this cup is the new testament in my blood: this do ye, as often as ye drink it, in remembrance of me.'
1 Cor. 11:24-25

COMMUNION SERVICE

'The cup of blessing which we bless, is it not the communion of the blood of Christ? The bread which we break, is it not the communion of the body of Christ?' 1 Cor. 10:16

Communion, also known as the LORD's Supper, was instituted the night the LORD took bread and wine in the upper room and celebrated the Passover. Although the Passover originated over 3500 years ago in the deliverance of Israel from Egypt, it symbolized our salvation from the world through the sacrificial death of Christ. The word 'communion' is used three times in Scripture: 1 Cor. 10:16; 2 Cor. 6:14; 13:14, and twice it refers to the Lord's Supper.

The Greek word for communion is koinonia, meaning: an intimate partnership, fellowship or intercourse. (Word Study). It also means to 'have in common, to 'share or participate.' It is also where we get the word 'commune.' Another connotation of communion means to 'exchange or interchange.' Each definition describes what Christ did for us on the cross. He entered into an intimate relationship with us; He shared in our suffering; He exchanged His royal estate for our poverty, and we become ONE with Him as we partake. Each of these meanings are encapsulated in the act of ingesting the bread and wine in memory of YESHUA.

Communion is not an obligation; it is a celebration of the Gospel! The Kingdom has come through the body and blood of Christ. He gave Himself to death to give us a new life, a clean start, and a renewed relationship with God. (1 Peter 3:18) It is not about a ritual to honor, but a GOD to worship. Adam died by eating; we live by eating.

"For I received from the Lord what I also delivered to you, that the Lord Jesus on the night when he was betrayed took bread, and when he had given thanks, he broke it, and said, "This is my body which is for you. Do this in remembrance of me." In the same way also he took the cup, after supper, saying, "This cup is the new covenant in my blood. Do this, as often as you drink it, in remembrance of me." **For as often as you eat this bread and drink the cup, you proclaim the Lord's death until He comes."** *(1 Cor. 11:23-26)*

History and Background Study

The history of Communion (the Lord's Supper), is an interesting study. The Old Testament exodus is the background for the Passover (seder) meal. The doorpost was smeared with the blood of the lamb that had been slain and eaten inside, symbolizing the body and the blood of the Lamb of God that was given for us. This Old Testament background is equally important in understanding the words and actions of Jesus at the 'last supper.' Below are a few notes. Research material is from Baker's Encyclopedia.

"This is my body." The actions of Jesus taking the bread are described similarly in Matt. (26:26), Mark (14:22), Luke (22:19), and 1 Cor. (11:23, 24). Jesus took the bread, gave thanks to God ("blessing" has the same meaning in the biblical context), and broke it. It is noteworthy that the same three actions are described in the records of the feeding of the 5000 and of the 4000 (Mk. 6:41; 8:6). What he said, according to all four accounts of the Last Supper was, "This is my body." What is clear is that in the taking of the bread there is the realization of Jesus' giving himself, his body to be broken on the cross, his life offered that we, in and through him, might have life. 1 Cor. 11:24 gives the words as *"This is my body, which is for you," and some early manuscripts have "broken for you."*
In Biblical thinking, "remembrance" often involves a realization and appropriation in the present of what has been done, or what has proven true in the past (e.g., Eccl. 12:1; Psa. 98:3; 106:45; 112:6; Isa. 57:11).

"This is my blood of the [new] covenant." When it came to the wine, Jesus took the cup, gave thanks, and handed it to his disciples for them to drink. In essence, the four accounts of the institution agree. Matt. 26:28 and Mk. 14:24 give the words of Jesus as *"This is my blood of the [new] covenant."* Luke 22:20 has *"This cup which is poured out for you is the new covenant in my blood,"* and 1 Cor.11:25 is similar to this. This refers back to the ritual of making a covenant offering the blood of a sacrifice. As with the covenant between God and Israel after the exodus. Implied also is that the prophetic hope of the new covenant (Jer. 31:31–34) was fulfilled in Jesus, as Heb. 8-9 describes.

"Poured out for many for the forgiveness of sins." The meaning of the death of Jesus as a sacrifice is linked to the understanding of the Passover and the covenant. It is also linked with Isaiah 53 in the Suffering Servant making himself "an offering for sin" (v 10). Luke 22:37 includes among the words of Jesus in the upper room the statement, "This Scripture must be fulfilled in me, 'And he was

reckoned with transgressors.'" That verse, Isa. 53:12, also says, "he poured out his soul to death" and "he bore the sin of many." Mk. 14:24 appears to allude to them when Jesus speaks of his blood poured out for many, and Matt. 26:28 adds 'for the forgiveness of sins.'

In Matt. 26:29 that future drinking of the fruit of the vine is said to be *"with you in my Father's kingdom."* In Luke 22:18, there are similar words, and three verses earlier the statement about fulfilling the Passover "in the kingdom of God." All of these can be understood as the ultimate realization of another hope that both OT and later Jewish apocalyptic writings set forward: the messianic banquet, the feast on the mountain of the Lord of which Isa. 25:6 speaks. In 1 Cor. 11:26 that future hope is quite explicitly that of Christ's second coming; for, says the apostle, "As often as you eat this bread and drink the cup, you proclaim the Lord's death until he comes."[1]

The Ceremony

Communion ceremony is where the congregation receives the bread and wine, representing the Body and Blood of our Lord and Savior Yeshua Jesus. We understand that the wine is not literal blood, nor the bread the literal body of Christ. We also understand that as the Lord was serving the bread and wine to his disciples, He distinctly said we are to eat and drink in *'remembrance'* of Him. Therefore, we realize that we are not literally ingesting Christ's flesh or blood (transubstantiation). However, we do believe in a literal manifestation of His presence during this sacred ceremony. To re-member can also mean to *'put back together.'* Christ's Body is being broken so that our bodies can be made whole. When we come together as the Body of Christ in communion, we're literally 'bringing His Body together.' We believe that Communion is not for the unbeliever because it celebrates a redemption that an unbeliever would not yet have experienced. How then shall we approach the Table of the Lord's Communion:
1. We must come with self-examination. *"But let a man examine himself, and so let him eat of that bread,"* 1 Cor. 11:28. It's not enough that others think we are fit to come, but we must examine ourselves. The Greek word "to examine" is a metaphor taken from the goldsmith who tries his metals in the fire. So before we come to the Lord's Table, we are to make a critical trial of ourselves by the Word.

---

[1] *Watson, Thomas (2010-04-27). The Mystery of the Lord's Supper*

Self-examination, being a reflexive act, is difficult. It is hard for a man to look inward and see the face of his own soul. The eye can see everything but itself. But this work is necessary because, if we do not examine ourselves, we are at a loss about our spiritual state. We don't know whether we are interested in the covenant or if we have a right to the seal.

2. We must come with a serious heart - When you come before the table of the Lord with a flippant spirit and lukewarm commitment to His work on the cross, you undermine the seriousness of the event. There should be a sense of unity, penitence, and seriousness when we approach the communion table.

3. We must come with an intelligent heart - If knowledge is lacking, it cannot be a reasonable service, Rom. 12:1. You must have a clear understanding of why you're partaking of the Lord's Supper. They that do not know the mystery do not feel the comfort. Pray for understanding that you may be able to discern.

4. **We must come with a loving heart -** The Love for the Lord should be our primary motivation for communion. Not a superficial religion but with the love that is birth out of gratitude and spiritual longing.He that's forgiven much, loves much.

5. **We must come with a repentant heart -** When we have sinned we should approach with our eyes filled with tears and our hearts washed in the waters of repentance. We must bring our brokenness which, though it is bitter to us, is sweet to Christ. *A broken Christ is to be received with a broken heart.*

THINGS TO REMIND THE PEOPLE DURING COMMUNION

The redemptive power of the Blood of Jesus.

The healing power of His broken body.

To meditate on the plan of God for mankind.

The power of His resurrection and the fellowship of His suffering.

The establishing of the New Covenant.

The Love of God.

TITHES AND OFFERINGS

TITHE

OLD TESTAMENT GIVING

NEW TESTAMENT GIVING

Each one must give as he has decided in his heart, not reluctantly or under compulsion, for God loves a cheerful giver.
2 Cor. 9:7

THE TITHE

'Give and it shall be given' Luke 6:38

God has a financial system that is designed to position His people to prosper and obtain material wealth. He has given instructions for us to established this system as stated in Scriptures through work ethics, guarded thinking, right relationships, and giving, which includes tithes and offerings.

What is the tithe? Tithe means the tenth part of anything or 10 percent. The words tithe and tithes appear over 36 times in Scripture. The rules concerning the tithe have changed through the centuries, but not its purpose. It was originally instituted by God before the Law of Moses. It is a matter of historical record that many other ancient nations (Sumer, for example) practiced some form of tithing in the early days of civilization. As the International Standard Bible Encyclopedia notes, tithing is a practice that is "ancient and deeply rooted in the history of the human race."

Abraham gave a tithe to the Melchizedek before the law. (Gen. 14) The tithe was allotted to the tribe of Levi. (Num. 18:24) God commanded the Levites to forfeit their inheritance and receive the benefits of the tithe from the other tribes. It is important that we understand the original intent for tithing and how GOD's Kingdom economic plan works today.

OLD TESTAMENT GIVING

The tithe was under the law and *not* optional under the Old Covenant. We know that the law was given as a testimony against Israel for the golden calf experience. The Law was Holy but was unable to make the people holy. The requirements of the law was insatiable. The paying of the tithe was also an act of worship, not just a duty. It was a privilege— a reasonable sacrifice, a giving back to God of a portion of that which He has given to His people. The tithe was considered to be a minimum standard, not the total of all giving. Most of all, the tithe was holy unto the Lord!

1. What was being tithed?
It was normally the 10th of the harvest of crops, livestocks, seed, honey, oil, wine, corn, herds, etc. And all the tithe of the herd or of the flock, whatever passes

under the herdsman's staff, by means of which each tenth animal as it passes through a small door is selected and marked.

Deut. 14:22 *'Thou shalt truly tithe **all the increase** of thy seed, that the field bring forth year by year. And thou shalt eat before the LORD thy God, in the place which he shall choose to place his name there, the tithe of thy corn, of thy wine, and of thine oil, and the firstlings of thy herds and of thy flocks; that thou mayest learn to fear the LORD thy God always.'*

Abraham paid tithes of the spoils to Melchizedek. (Gen,14:20)

Jacob made a deal with God saying, 'IF you give me... I will give you a tithe of all.' (Gen. 28:22) (Not of compulsion. Not because I have to.)

So, we find that the tithe is not just from crops and livestock. In fact, if someone wanted to redeem crops or livestock (change for cash), he had to add another 20% to the gift. (Lev. 27:31)

2. Who receives the tithe?

Tithes were given to the priest and also to the poor. God told Moses to set aside the tribe of Levi to become workers of the tabernacle and priests to offer sacrifices for the people. God was their inheritance, and the other tribes were to pay their tithes to the Levites.

Num. 18:21 *And, behold, I have given the children of Levi all the tenth in Israel for an inheritance, for their service which they serve, even the service of the tabernacle of the congregation.*

Heb. 7:5 *'And verily they that are of the sons of Levi, who receive the office of the priesthood, have a commandment to take tithes of the people according to the law, that is, of their brethren, though they come out of the loins of Abraham:'*

Deut. 26:12 *'I have given it to the Levite, the sojourner, the fatherless, and the widow, according to all your commandment that you have commanded me. I have not transgressed any of your commandments, nor have I forgotten them.'*

3. When were the tithes given?

The tithes were given at three different times as stated in Scripture.

(1) An **annual tithe,** to be paid towards the support of the Levites and priests. who were not allowed an inheritance of their own and thus were at the mercy of the state (**Num. 18:21–24**).

(2) A separate **annual feast tithe**, which went towards the expenses and upkeep of the Temple, and the various feasts and sacrifices surrounding it. (Deut. 14:22)

(3) **A third-year tithe** for the poor of the land, and again for the Levite. (Deut. 26:12-15)

'Come to Bethel, and transgress; at Gilgal multiply transgression; and bring your sacrifices every morning, and your tithes after three years:' (Amos 4:4)

NEW TESTAMENT GIVING

The tithe was originally under the Law. The Law was given to reveal sin in the flesh that we should obey it until the coming Redeemer. The Law could not make us holy in that it was weak because of the flesh. The cross of Christ put an end to the Law. We now have the Holy Spirit to change our character to righteous. The Blood of Jesus changed everything. The Book of the Covenant of Promise was not the Law of Moses. Under the Old Covenant, giving was a law! However, the way we give has changed. Yeshua Jesus spoke these words:

Luke 6:38 *Give, and it shall be given unto you; good measure, pressed down, and shaken together, and running over, shall men give into your bosom. For with the same measure that ye mete withal it shall be measured to you again.*

Matt. 6:1-4 *"Take heed that ye do not your alms before men, to be seen of them: otherwise ye have no reward of your Father which is in heaven… and thy Father which see in secret himself shall reward thee openly."*

Does this Scripture give you the idea that Jesus has altered the regulations for giving? Although this is alms which is directed to the poor, it could also refer to the widow, fatherless, orphan who were also receivers of the tithe.

Again, Jesus sitting at the place of the offerings notices a widow who gave 2 mites. (100%)   (Luke 21:1-4) He compared her giving to the rich who were casting their gifts into the treasury. He said that the widow gave more because she gave from her lack. If she had given a tithe, it would have been relatively equal to the wealthy. This is the difference between Law giving and giving under Grace. The Apostle Paul brings another perspective about giving. Paul shows us how to give in the church age and never mention the tithe under the law. You may be surprised to find out that God actually requires us to give more than the tithe.

2 Cor. 9:6-7 *'The point is this: whoever sows sparingly will also reap sparingly, and whoever sows bountifully will also reap bountifully.*

7 Each one must give as he has decided in his heart, not reluctantly or under compulsion, for God loves a cheerful giver.'

UNDER THE POWER OF GRACE YOU GIVE MORE!

The tithe was a command for you to give under penalty of the law. Grace giving is a choice with a blessing attached. The same way that the Spirit of God will compel your walk of righteousness, He will also compel your giving! This is why God loves a cheerful giver, because it would be the result of what you've **purposed in your heart (compelled by the Spirit).**

When you see the true message here, you will understand how the cross of Christ has effected the tithe. The frequency of giving never changed. God still requires that we sow and give as God has prospered you. BUT, the amount has possibly changed. God is not only requiring 10%, He may also compel you to give 30, 50, or even !00%. It is good to use the tithe (10%) as your guideline. It's okay to give a tenth of your increase. But, that is actually the least that you should give. The tithe is the spiritual exercise for your finances, just as there are spiritual disciplines for every area of your life. It is God's desire that you walk in Kingdom wealth and SONSHIP!

THE GRACE GIVING FOR KINGDOM BLESSINGS!

The tithe is directly connected to the instructions (Torah) that were given to Israel to governed every aspect of their lives. (ie., diet, clothing, children, relationships, work ethics, worship, business ethics, and Giving). When they gave the tithe, God gave them credit for the whole. The tithe was the power to get wealth and to partner with God in financing His covenant plan. (Deut. 8:18)

Preachers that attack the tithe are not learned. They may be attempting to destroy a legalistic yoke; unfortunately, it is the one that connects us to Kingdom finances and blessings. We don't have to tithe… We get to tithe!

LEADERSHIP

MEASURE OF RULE

FIVE-FOLD MINISTRY

EIGHT TESTS OF LEADERS

AUTHORITY

'Let all things be done decently and in order.'
1 Cor. 14:40

MEASURE OF RULE

Let every soul be subject to the governing authorities. For there is no authority except from God, and the authorities that exist are appointed by God.   Rom. 13:1

It is a fact that no congregation can rise above the level of its Leadership. Churches can rise and fall based solely on the effectiveness of its Leaders. The problem with the description of church leadership today is that its base more on business principles than Scripture. Today, pastors are like heads of corporations, and church programs are marketing strategies. The practices of business executives take priority over the guidelines of the Word of God. Many of our churches have become lifeless organizations with administrative methods that have replaced the spiritual principles of God's Word. This deviation may be the cause of many of the people of God becoming scattered in their commitment and indifferent to spiritual authority.   But, God is raising leaders after His own heart that will feed His sheep and build His Church.

Although the Church must conduct business, it is certainly not a business. The operation of the Lord is like night and day to the business practices of the world. Its leaders are not corporate heads, but servants. Its finances are increased, not by what it receives, but by what it gives. And its promotions are not earned but rather bestowed by God. The Kingdom of Heaven is our pattern. God's plan is to establish His Kingdom on the Earth through the Body of Christ!

Pastors, however, must have business savvy. God has set up a company of leaders (and soldiers), each with a distinct measure of governmental rule. A *'measure of rule'* is an area or extent in which one has jurisdiction or authority. Measure of rule is important because it establishes order. Without it, there would be chaos, confusion, disrespect for authority and disregard for people with experience.

LEADERSHIP

The definition of 'lead' is to show someone the way to a destination by going in front of or beside them. Leadership is the action of leading a group or an organization. Leaders are born, (and made) in the Body of Christ. But, unlike the world system, leadership in the Church does not mean lordship. (1 Pet. 5:1-3) The erroneous division termed 'clergy and laity' has caused a division that is not at all in the plan of God. In the NT church, there were two distinct categories of ministry. They were never referred to as 'clergy and laity.' The two distinctions were 'governmental and congregational' differing in function but not of lesser or greater importance.

Although there was a difference in their functions, all Christians were considered ministers. This false idea of 'clergy and laity,' 'us vs. them' has become prevalent in the minds of believers today. Yeshua Jesus has a Kingdom, and He ALONE is King! He has established Pastors who are subordinate governors, under-shepherds, who have been given charge of His sheep and His Vision. The Pastor who rules well, will not rule in an arbitrary way according to their will, but according to the Mind of Christ with all faithfulness, humility, wisdom, sagacity (shrewdness), and diligence.

With that said, we must also understand the importance of Leadership in the Church. We're living in times when God-given leaders are being displaced, disrespected, sabotaged and discouraged. God has a problem with that! (Psa. 105:15) We are to honor leaders and esteem them with respect. (1 Thess. 5:12) God takes it very seriously when leaders experience verbal, spiritual, or physical attacks. God has placed leaders to govern and guide the Body of Christ and bring them to His desired end. Leaders are selected and called by God, and not by man.

CHURCH HISTORY

Pentecost (50 days after the crucifixion and 10 days after the ascension of Christ) marks the birth of the church. At this point, Peter emerged as the spokesperson. The other decisive leader of the apostolic church was Paul, in whose life three great ancient traditions intersected. Religiously, he was a Jew, culturally a Greek, and politically a Roman.

By the end of the first century, the death of the apostles produced a leadership vacuum in the Church. Who had the authority to lead the believers? The Church Fathers filled the gap. As a term of affection and esteem, "father" was generally given to spiritual leaders of the Church (known as elders or bishops). The Fathers can be divided into three groups: 1) Apostolic Fathers (a.d. 95–150), wrote what was devotional and edifying in nature. 2) Apologists (a.d. 150–300) wrote literature that defended the faith and countered error. 3) Theologians (a.d. 300–600) began doing systematic theology. In Church history, the medieval church comprised the period from about 600 to 1517.

Martin Luther in Oct 1517, nailed 95 theses on the church door declaring Justification by faith in Christ. The Enlightenment, John Locke's empiricism, affirmed the basic goodness of man, no doctrine of innate evil, or original sin. In 1806, The Haystack Prayer Meeting launched the missionary movement in America. By the 18th Century, a revival called the First Great Awakening, with the revivalistic and evangelistic preaching of Charles Finney (1792–1875). The Layman's Prayer Revival of 1858 Praying, not preaching, sparked the movement that started in a noonday prayer meeting in New York. By the 1950s, fundamentalist Protestantism was rife with tension. Leaders sought to reform fundamentalism to be more scholarly and to put more emphasis on apologetics and the social dimension of Christianity. They founded Fuller Theological Seminary.

On April 9, 1906, the Azusa Street Revival began. It was a historic Pentecostal revival meeting that took place in Los Angeles, California and is the origin of the Pentecostal movement. It was led by William J. Seymour, an African-American preacher. The revival was characterized by ecstatic spiritual experiences accompanied by amazing physical healing miracles, dramatic worship services, speaking in tongues, and inter-racial mingling. The participants were criticized by the secular media and Christian theologians for behaviors considered to be outrageous and unorthodox, especially at the time. Today, the revival is considered by historians to be the catalyst for the spread of Pentecostalism in the 20th Century.

Many existing Wesleyan-holiness denominations adopted the Pentecostal message, such as the Church of God, the Church of God in Christ, and the Pentecostal Holiness Church. The formation of new denominations also occurred, motivated by doctrinal differences between Wesleyan Pentecostals and their Finished Work counterparts, such as the Assemblies of God formed in 1914 and the Pentecostal Church of God formed in 1919. An early doctrinal controversy led to a split between Trinitarian and Oneness Pentecostals; the latter founded the Pentecostal Assemblies of the World in 1916. There are more than 500 million Pentecostal and charismatic believers across the globe, and it is the fastest-growing form of Christianity today.[1]

---

[1]Eckman, J. P. (2002). *Exploring church history* (p. 4). Wheaton, IL: Crossway.

FIVE-FOLD MINISTRY

*'And **HE** gave the apostles, the prophets, the evangelists, the shepherds and teachers, to **equip** the saints for the work of ministry, for building up the body of Christ, Till we all come in the unity of the faith, and of the knowledge of the Son of God, …' Eph. 4:11-13 (ESV)*

According to Greek grammar, the five kinds of gifted people are listed in the *'predicate accusative'*, which implies that Christ *'gave some to be.'* R. Bratcher , *a noted theologian wrote:*

The Greek "he himself gave some as apostles," etc., could be understood to mean *'he appointed some to be'* since the gifts are properly the offices or responsibilities in the church and not the persons as such (so NEB "some to be," etc.). The statement 'he appointed some to be' may be rendered as "he chose some to be." But, often a more appropriate rendering is equivalent to "to some he gave the task of being …" or "… assigned the task of being …"[1]

Apostles - The Greek word a*póstolos* means "one sent as an authoritative delegate." The apostles have many assignments including, set doctrine, cover ministries, and are foundational in establishing local churches.

Prophets - The mouthpiece of God. Prophets spoke by a Divine utterance to the people to provide edification, exhortation, and comfort. (1 Cor. 14:3) The prophets also gave God's warnings and judgements. They predict future events.

Evangelists - Those who engaged in spreading the gospel, going from place to place similar to present-day missionaries.

Pastors and Teachers - These two are listed together because of the definite article "the" occurs before "pastors" but not before "teachers"… and because the word "and" (kai) differs from the other "and's" (de) in the verse. The Pastor is the set man or woman in a congregation whose given the responsibility and the authority to protect, nurture and teach the people of God. They were formally called overseers, bishops or shepherds, as they had a hands-on relationship with the flock of Christ. All pastors are teachers, but not all teachers are pastors! (See 'Bible Knowledge Commentary')

---

[1] Bratcher, R. G., & Nida, E. A. (1993). *A handbook on Paul's letter to the Ephesians* (p. 101). New York:

Leaders are God's gifts given to train and equip the Body of Christ for the work of ministry! Not all are governmental ministers, but all are servants. The modern clergy/laity mentality and the concept of salvation as a product instead of a relationship have crippled the church.

The five-fold ministry assignment is clearly described in Ephesians 4:11-13.

"to equip the saints" - The term "equip" means <u>to cause something to be ready for its assigned purpose.</u>

"for the building up of the body of Christ" Paul mixes his building metaphor with his body metaphor. The focus is not on the individual, but on the body.

"until we all attain" The Greek tense is an aorist active subjunctive. It literally means "to arrive at a destination." Note that 'ALL' refers to our corporate responsibility. Notice the three aspects of maturity mentioned: (1) unity of the faith, (2) knowledge of the Son of God; and (3) Christ-like maturity.

"the knowledge" This is the compound Greek term *epi-ginōskō*, which implies a full experiential knowledge. This was an obvious rejection of the gnostic false teachers' emphasis on secret, exclusive knowledge. The believers' knowledge is complete in Christ.

"mature man" This is in contrast to "children" (huios). The Greek root (*telos*) means "complete," "fully equipped." (KJV)

AUTHORITY (Three Levels)

Ecclesiastical - Ecclesiastical authority is determined by ones Spiritual prowess, assignment and experience. It should never be based upon familiarity or age.

Corporate - Corporate authority is determined and assigned by the Pastor, (i.e., the head of an auxiliary) and is based upon one's abilities, gifts and/or talents.

Appointed - Appointed authority is delegated for a particular assignment.

One may be the leader of an auxiliary, i.e., Corporate authority, and yet be subject to one that's under their leadership that has Ecclesiastical authority. For example, an Evangelist working under an auxiliary leader who is not a minister. By the same token, someone with Ecclesiastical authority must respect and submit to one having Corporate authority over them. In the event of a special occasion, the Pastor (or a leader), may give a person temporary delegated authority to accomplish a task or a particular assignment.

EIGHT TESTS OF LEADERS

TIME TEST - In the Time test, by all outward appearances, God does not seem to be fulfilling the word He gave a leader in the past. The Time test will try a leader's patience, forcing him/her to trust God to fulfill his call and ministry in His own time and way. This test gives the leader an opportunity to grow in faith. Every leader has a measure of trust and confidence in God. Because each must lead people to believe in God for every detail of life, however, a leader must be given more faith with which to strengthen his own people. The Time test also purifies a leader's motives and attitudes. During times of delay, a leader can see how their own impure, selfish or proud motives and attitudes can cloud their desires before the Lord. God proves Himself to be a miracle-working, faithful God to everyone He has called to the service of His kingdom. Many times a leader believes that their own activity and striving can fulfill God's vision for His Church. During the Time test, when men's plans can only fail, God arranges a miracle to bring all of the glory to Himself. As He does the miracle, He demonstrates His faithfulness to His leaders.

CHARACTER TEST - In the Character test, the leader is surrounded by ungodliness that attempts to pull him/her in its direction. The leader may be tempted to sin through the lust of the flesh, the lust of the eyes, or the pride of life. In order to develop leaders with strong, godly character qualities--love, joy, peace, patience, self-control, faithfulness--God puts His leaders in fiery places so they may learn to stand strong in Him. Purpose. The Character test shows to the leader the areas of weakness in his own personality. When God brings a situation into a leader's life which requires much patience, he realizes he must call on more of God's grace. An area of need usually surfaces, where he must allow God to work. Every leader has hidden character deficiencies of which he is totally unaware, until confronted with a specific situation that demands a godly response. To expose his own true inward self to every leader, God uses the Character Test. The Character test also motivates a leader to stand up boldly against the powers of darkness around him. Too many leaders are shy about proclaiming the truth. Too many wait until they are attacked from outside before they take the initiative of preaching the gospel. Many need to be confronted with evil so they will stand up boldly for the name of the Lord and His righteousness.

MOTIVATION TEST - This is a heavenly "examination" in which God exposes to the leader what inner and outer forces influence his decision-making processes. God will arrange situations to reveal a leader's true hidden intentions, thoughts, values, and priorities that cause her to make choices or act in a certain way. A leader may not always know why he/she does something. What appears to motivate you, from an outer inspection, may be far from your real internal motives. God uses the Motivation test to reveal those inner drives and to purify your desires for the glory of God, the salvation of souls, and the edification of the Church. A leader may serve God for what they can get out of God, rather than what they can give to Him or His people. A minister may use their gifts to glorify themselves, rather than God. God puts His leaders through Motivation Tests to expose unrighteous drives, and then to replace them with motives of His Spirit, and true love out of a pure heart.

THE SERVANT TEST - In the Servant test, a minister is asked to do menial tasks that seem below their high calling in God. No menial work is below any true servant of God. But especially before (or even during) the time of fully giving him/herself to prayer and the Word instead of *"waiting on tables"* (see Acts 6:2), God tests a leader to see if they are willing to do menial service. The Servant Test reveals whether a ministry's motivation is simply to be in the public eye and receive service, or if you truly desires to help and serve. Those in authority over that ministry *(we use the word "ministry" to refer to a person who ministers)* will see how well they pass the test. God may instruct authorities over a ministry to use this test to discern the minister's commitment to service. Does a minister think it below their ministry to sweep the church floor? Does a minister believe it is beneath her calling to sing with others and not to solo? These are revealing questions. This test also shows to God's called governmental ministries what it feels like to do different jobs in the church. You can appreciate the effort and time a person cleaning the church puts in when you experience some of it Yourself? Every leader needs personal experience in different jobs in the Church, so they can better understand and communicate with people in those positions.

WILDERNESS TEST - In the Wilderness test, God guides a leader into a materially and/or spiritually dry and desolate place when no fruit comes from her life or ministry. In such times, a leader wonders whether they really received a call of God upon his/her life, because he/she appears to have no direct involvement in the building and work of the kingdom of God. Sometimes, a leader is left with no one else to talk to but God. The Wilderness test increases a leader's appreciation for the good things that God has already put in his/her life. This test also teaches the leader how to discern whether the Lord alone sustains their spiritual life. Does a leader's prayer life, the study of the Word and evangelism activities drop off just because they are not in "full-time" ministry? God also uses the Wilderness test to strip the leader of all the wisdom and ways of the world to teach the ways of His Spirit. Every leader must learn that God's ways are different from their ways. The Wilderness test motivates a leader to seek the Lord in a consistent life of prayer and the Word, to find the true source of strength: God Himself.

DISCOURAGEMENT TEST - A leader is going through the Discouragement test when you allow circumstances or people to discourage you and dampen your faith and courage in the Lord. A discouraged leader can be deterred from an assignment which he/she believed was God's will. During such times, a minister may lose their confidence or hope in God, His provision, His promises, or His calling. Discouragement causes the leader to go to God in prayer. The Psalms express most of the different conditions of heart that people face during their lifetime. The moods of the Psalms vary from joy over the defeat of enemies to the sorrow and depths of despair and discouragement. During the Discouragement Test, a leader should try to find the Psalm(s) that best express the mood of his/her soul, and then pray through it to God. Discouraging times of stress and trial are not wrong. But the attitude you have during those difficult circumstances can be, if you continue with self-pity or feelings of discouragement. A leader must learn through these times that your joy comes from delighting in the Lord, not delighting only in happy circumstances or positive responses from people. No leader will sustain his/her ministry without learning how to get total joy and peace directly and solely from God. The Discouragement test also reveals the hidden, bad attitudes in a leader. Many leaders can rejoice in the Lord when everything is going the way they think things should. But how many allow themselves to complain and murmur when things go unexpectedly the other way? During discouragement, the Lord allows the leader to uncover poor attitudes in himself, for which he/she must ask God to forgive and cleanse.

WARFARE TEST - The Warfare test happens when a leader encounters violent spiritual opposition to his progress in the Spirit, or in her extending of God's kingdom. Though it happens in the realm of the spirit, it can find natural expressions in conflicts with people, lack of response to your ministry, or inner struggles (including the feeling of unbearable temptation to sin). Some people think anointed leaders can't be tempted like other people can. The Bible says that even Jesus "was in all points tempted like as we are, yet without sin" (Hebrews 4: 15). The calling of God does not remove human susceptibility to temptation. Leaders must make a conscious effort to *"walk in the Spirit and ye shall not fulfill the lusts of the flesh" (Galatians 5: 16).* Spiritual warfare forces the leader to grow stronger in the Spirit. In this, the spiritual realm is like the natural realm, where a muscle becomes stronger only through exercise and resistance. *Hebrews 5:14 uses the word "exercise" when it states that solid spiritual food is for the mature, "who by reason of use have their senses exercised to discern both good and evil."* Some leaders are not mature because they do not train or exercise their spiritual senses enough. Through spiritual warfare, a leader learns how to use effectively their spiritual weapons of the Word, prayer, worship, and the name of Yeshua Jesus.

USAGE TEST - A leader undergoes the Usage test in his or her life or ministry preparation when you cannot find the need, demand, opportunity, invitation, results or expected occasion to exercise your ministry. "Put on the shelf" is a common description for this situation. God may put a leader "on the shelf" temporarily for several reasons. First, God may desire to show the leader that you depends too much on your actual anointing or talent, rather than upon the Lord Himself. Being "on the shelf" may stimulate you to develop your personal prayer and life in the Word for more than ministry success. God may desire to humble you. A leader who is greatly used of God can become proud and self-sufficient. It is simply human nature to credit men for being the source of their strengths, especially their obvious ones. The Usage test also gives God an opportunity to purify the motives of His leaders. What causes a leader to act or speak the way they do? The Usage test may also deepen the message of the leader. Many leaders live on their past sermons and messages without getting fresh words or experiences from God. Some leaders stay so busy that they either do not have, or do not take the time to deepen their messages. But, the people of God cannot constantly feed from the same old messages without growing emaciated and hungry for more. God must sometimes put a minister out of public commission for a while so that they will be motivated to deepen his/her understanding of the Word of God.

(See "The Makings of a Leader" by Frank Damazio[1] for the complete list of God's testings of a leader)

Scriptures for LEADERSHIP

Heb. 13:7 Remember your leaders, those who spoke to you the word of God. Consider the outcome of their way of life, and imitate their faith.

1 Pet. 5:1-3 The elders who are among you I exhort... Shepherd the flock of God which is among you, serving as overseers, neither by compulsion... nor as being lords over those entrusted to you, but being examples to the flock.

1 Thess. 5:12 And we beseech you, brethren, to know them which labor among you, and are over you in the Lord, and admonish you; And to esteem them very highly in love for their work's sake. And be at peace among yourselves.

1 Tim. 3:5 For if a man does not know how to rule his own house, how will he take care of the church of God?

1 Tim. 5:17 Let the elders who rule well be counted worthy of double honor, especially those who labor in the word and doctrine.

Heb. 13:17 Obey those who rule over you, and be submissive, for they watch out for your souls, as those who must give account. Let them do so with joy and not with grief, for that would be unprofitable for you.

1 Thess. 5:25 Brethren, pray for us.

---

[1]"The Makings of a Leader" by Frank Damazio

WEDDINGS

PREPARATION

WEDDING PLACEMENT

WEDDING CEREMONY

'Wherefore they are no more twain, but one flesh. What therefore God hath joined together, let not man put asunder.'   *Matt. 19:6*

THE WEDDING

'What therefore God hath joined together, let not man put asunder.' Mark 10:9

The marriage ceremony is one of the most sacred of all rituals that a minister conducts. It's never merely a social event, but is always a rite in which a man and a woman enter into a sacred covenant ordain and sustain by God. Jesus chose that occasion to perform His first miracle. In keeping with that ceremony it should be the desire of every minister to make every wedding a memorable, beautiful, and meaningful event.

WEDDING PREPARATION - Many ministers require **at least two** prenuptial counseling sessions with the bride and groom, one to discuss the wedding and the other to discuss the marriage. I personally like to have **at least four sessions**, one with each partner alone in addition to the other two sessions.

1st Counsel with the bride - 2nd Counsel with the groom.

Discuss subjects such as: family finances, step children relationships, in-law relations, religious differences, personality differences, and their individual vision for the future. The sexual side of marriage should be thoroughly discussed. The couple should be reminded that the wedding will only last about 30 minutes. But, marriage will last a lifetime. Both need to be prayerfully planned.

3rd Session with bride and groom together - This is a detailed discussion about the Scriptural position governing marriage. This is where you allow them to talk about the obvious challenges and strengths of their union. You also use this time to help them personalize their vows. Offer prayer, biblical principles, and encouragement to help them over come any unforeseen pitfalls.

4th Session is to discuss the ceremony - Deciding on attendees, appropriate music, favorite Scriptures, length of service, added services, and family placement, etc. This is also where they determine if relationships between divorced parents are such that an extra row should separate the father of the bride and his wife from the mother of the bride (and her husband). In some weddings, the minister is often called on to direct the rehearsal. It is better if you suggest a 'qualified' close friend or a paid consultant to be used. This allows that person to direct both the rehearsal and the wedding.

Never surrender the spiritual atmosphere of the wedding service to anyone. You must provide all instructions for the ceremony.

THE UNEXPECTED

Be prepared for the unexpected because brides and grooms are nervous. Fainting or nausea is a possibility. Rings are sometimes dropped. Vows may be misstated. Even you (the minister), might make a mistake, i.e., the MINISTER DOESN'T HAVE THE MARRIAGE LICENSE.

Professional photographers must not take flash photos during the ceremony. You can't always control wedding guests who pop up from a pew to take their own iPhone shot even though it is rude and disruptive. Suggest a video recording of the wedding. Everything possible should be done to make the wedding as memorable and comfortable as possible.

LEGALITIES

You must understand your legal responsibilities. They vary from state to state. Your local county court clerk can provide you with this information. Be sure you understand any domicile requirements about where the marriage license is to be purchased and where the ceremony can be performed. If you travel to a different state to perform a wedding, make sure you meet the qualifications in that state. [1]

It is a good idea to have the marriage license brought to you at the rehearsal or before the wedding. You should not perform a wedding unless you have the marriage license in your possession. After the ceremony, sign the marriage license and mail it to the appropriate court clerk as soon as possible.

THE WEDDING PLACEMENT

Forty-five minutes before the wedding begins, the music is played softly and the ushers greet and seat the people as they arrive.

Five minutes before the ceremony begins, the candles are lit. They may be lit earlier if the lighting is not a part of the ceremony.

Two minutes before the ceremony begins, the father and mother of the groom are seated on the second row on the right. (See Diagram).

---

[1]The New Ministers Manual <"http://www.baylor.edu/content/services/document.php?id=146523">

One minute before the ceremony begins, the mother of the bride is seated on the second row on the left. (See Diagram)

Step-parents are normally in attendance and should be given the same courtesies as grandparents which are usually seated near the front of the church behind the parents. If a divorced father is giving his daughter in marriage and his present wife is in attendance, she should be seated prior to the mother of the groom and behind the row on which the mother of the bride is seated.

Minister

Maid of Honor   **Groom/Best Man**

Bride's side   **Groom's side**

Bride - Dad

If the Dad of the bride is deceased or divorced, the bride may choose a stepfather, brother, uncle, or even a friend to give her in marriage.

At the appointed time to begin, the special music is played and the minister, the groom, and best man come in together and face the audience.

Then the groomsmen and the bridesmaids enter down the aisle, followed by the maid of honor. Small pieces of tape on the floor may be used to mark where the they are to stand.

The bride enters on the left arm of her father (or whoever is giving her away). The congregation stand as the bride enters.

The bride and her father walk to the front of the audience and stop. The minister then asks, "Who gives this woman to be married?" The father replies, "Her mother and I do" (or simply I do if the mother is not present).

The father kisses the bride on the cheek, hands her to the groom and is seated.

The groom takes the bride and steps up before the minister.

When the ceremony is over, **the bride and groom lead the recessional**.

The parents of the bride follow, then the parents of the groom. Grandparents may also be escorted out if they are present followed by step-parents. The minister may invite the guests to the reception before dismissing the congregation.

THE WEDDING CEREMONY

We are gathered here in the sight of God and the presence of these witnesses to join together in holy matrimony _____. (If there is anyone who would object to this union, let them speak now or forever hold their peace.) You are here today to make one of the most important decisions in your life and that is to spend the rest of your lives together. You're not here to make promises, but to enter into a covenant. One of the most sacred of all covenants because it exemplifies Christ and His Church. Marriage, like all covenants, involves an exchange; exchange of love, exchange of commitment and exchange of family. When you enter this covenant you will no longer be two, but One… One in Spirit, One in Mind, One in Purpose. This covenant has the power to keep you together if you keep the covenant. And what God has joined together let no man put asunder. If you understand the importance of the steps you're about take, and if you vow to keep the sanctity of this covenant, you may turn and face each other and prepare to exchange your marriage vows.

_____ Do you solemnly swear to love, honor, and cherish _____. To care for him/her and keep him/her in sickness and in health; for richer or for poorer; for better or for worse as long as you both shall live. (Repeat for Groom) Is there a ring? This ring is a symbol of this eternal covenant which is never to be broken. It's a symbol of the cycles of life that you will grow through and the union that will stand the test of time… also never to be broken.

_____ Take this ring, hold her/his left hand, look into her/his eyes and repeat after me. _____ I promise to love you, honor, and respect you. I promise to be with you always… in good times and in bad times, I will never leave your side. I promise to keep myself for you only forsaking All others. I pledge my loyalty and life to you And with this ring, I thee wed. (Repeat for Bride)

As you have faced each other and exchanged your vows, you are to alway look to one another for love, for encouragement, for support— not to family, not to friends, but to each other — and to GOD. If you promise before God to keep these vows as conditions of this covenant as long as you both shall live, please indicate by saying, "I will."   By the power vested in me by the state of Nevada, and as a minister of the gospel by God, I now pronounce you husband and wife. You may kiss your bride.

(Ceremony used by Dr. Glories Powell)

My Wedding Message

FUNERALS

PREPARATION

ORDER OF SERVICE

EULOGY

GRAVESIDE SERVICE

Yea, though I walk through the valley of the shadow of death, I will fear no evil; For You are with me; Your rod and Your staff, they comfort me.

Psa. 23:4

FUNERAL PREPARATION

'For I know that my Redeemer lives, and at the last he will stand upon the earth. And after my skin has been thus destroyed, yet in my flesh I shall see God.' Job 19:25-25

There are few times when your presence will be more needed and appreciated, and when you will be able to touch people more, than when there is a death. People will forget the sermons you preach, the ministry you've built, or the degrees you have. But they will never forget that you came, and how you helped them in a time of grief when there was a death of a loved one. Being with people and ministering to them during their time of mourning builds bonds that last a lifetime. This is normally for a Pastor. But, even as a Minister, you have the responsibility to extend the same care and concern to a hurting family. What do you do when someone dies?

- **Call the home** as soon as you hear of the death and ask when would be a convenient time to visit. Unless a specific time is stated, go immediately if possible. For many people, you represent God. Your presence will be a source of strength and comfort to them. And they need you.

- **What will you say** when you get there? It will always be a struggle with what to say. A warm handshake, a gentle hug, a pat on the shoulder, and the simple words, "God bless you, (name)," is enough. Words mean very little. Above all, avoid trite and empty explanations. Your presence is enough. It says, "I care." It says, "God cares." It says, "You matter." It says, "You are not alone. We are here to help you through this."

- **Listen.** Let the person talk and try to remember what they say about the deceased. Write them down as soon as you leave. They will give you important information about the life and the death of the deceased. Information that you may be able to mention in the funeral sermon to make it more personal.

- **You don't need** to stay long—15-30 minutes is sufficient.

- **When the time is right,** ask if you can lead in prayer. After the prayer assure the family that you will be available to talk about funeral arrangements.

EULOGY

The eulogy is a message or sermon prepared for the home going celebration. It is the formal expression of praise for the dearly departed. The Greek word 'eulogia' is translated 'eu = good' and 'logia = words.' The opening of the eulogy is not quite like preaching a Sunday message. In fact, because it is so personal, it is geared toward the departed and the family.

Giving a eulogy isn't easy, but it's something you'll never regret doing. It's okay to feel some nervousness and apprehension, but remember that people have come to grieve and honor this individual -- and you are there to help them do that. You are also there because they trust you to do the job.

When you write the eulogy, think about your personal experience with the individual. If it has been minimal, take the notes you have from talking to the family and friends of the deceased. Include details and anecdotes that will help to describe their philosophy of life and their unique way of moving through the world. Avoid clichés, generalities, and passive language. Reading your first draft aloud will help you identify gaps and misstatements, clear up any areas of confusion, and improve the flow.[1] *"This is called a memorial service because we've gathered today to remember...to bring to mind, the good times, the happy times, the hope filled times, the victories as well as the challenges of (name)."*

If you have performance anxiety, delivering the eulogy may be the hardest part of the whole experience. Try to remember that you're speaking to a friendly audience. This isn't an audition, a popularity contest, or your day in court. Your audience is full of people who cared about the person. You'll probably find that your nervousness gradually subsides once your message has begun. You may be tempted to rush through a reading, but try to resist. Read slowly, and pause briefly between verses and at the end of any story or poem. Take a glass of water

---

[1]"How to Deliver a Eulogy' Delivering a Eulogy <https://www.caring.com/articles/how-to-deliver-a-eulogy>

with you to the podium, in case your mouth feels dry, and remind yourself to breathe. Look up between sentences. If you find that making eye contact with individuals in the audience is distracting, focus on a point in the back of the room. Don't worry if you become choked up or your voice is shaky; no one will judge you for your expression of emotion.

Eulogy Do's and Don'ts

•Don't go on too long. Keep the eulogy succinct and to the point.

•Try to stick to the eulogy you wrote and practiced. Unless you're an experienced speaker, adding a new idea at the last minute may cause you to lose the train of thought and begin to ramble.

•Be careful with humor. Although a few jokes can lighten the tone of a memorial service, inappropriate or excessive humor can offend. Remember that you're not there to roast the person or other guests, and that feelings are likely to be more fragile than usual.

•Remember that it's a eulogy, not a chance to settle scores. If you have unsettling information about the deceased, keep it out of the eulogy. A memorial service is not the time to introduce any negative surprises.

•Don't be too hard on yourself. If the eulogy, or your delivery of it, doesn't go over as well as you'd hoped, try not to think of it as a failure. It's difficult to be at your most creative and eloquent when you just preached a funeral. If you deliver the eulogy with as much sincerity and feeling as you can, it will do the job of memorializing the person, comforting the mourners, and providing you the chance to say what GOD has given you.

GRAVESIDE

Ecclesiastes 7:1 A good name is better than precious ointment, and the day of death than the day of birth. Matthew 5:4 "Blessed are those who mourn, for they shall be comforted... " (Jesus' words)

WHAT TO DO AT THE CEMETERY-

When the casket has been placed over the grave and the family seated, the minister may say: We have now done all we can do for our friend, (deceased). *"We have brought his/her body to its final resting place. We now commend their body to the earth from whence it came. From dust to dust, from ashes to ashes."*

Read again from the word of God. Some appropriate passages are:

Psa. 23; 1 Thess. 4:13-18; Rev. 21:1-7, or Psa. 1.

You may then ask the people to bow for prayer and say: "This prayer will conclude the services."

Following the prayer, shake hands with family members and move out from under the canopy.

Honorarium - If you're going to receive an honorarium or stipend for performing the service, be discreet and not obvious. Many times the family is consumed or preoccupied and paying you may not be foremost on their minds. It's okay to leave your card with a prominent family member or with someone that you've been assisting with the planning. You may also settle this before the funeral and make sure that there is an 'understood' agreement on the amount. You don't want to have money be the bitter taste in an otherwise memorable service.

Remember: God called you, not people! Whatever we do is as unto the LORD.

ORDINATION
&
License

SERVICE AND REQUIREMENTS

'The Spirit of the LORD shall rest upon Him, The Spirit of wisdom and understanding, The Spirit of counsel and might, The Spirit of knowledge and of the fear of the LORD.'

Isa. 11:2

ORDINATIONS

'...and he gave some, apostles; and some, prophets; and some, evangelists; and some, pastors and teachers; For the perfecting of the saints, for the work of the ministry, for the edifying of the body of Christ...'   *Eph. 4:11-12*

CODA MINISTRIES' Ordination service celebrates the consecration of a man or woman as one who is called to full or part time Ministry. It is a service of praise and thanksgiving to GOD for the impartation of the Divine gift and calling. It includes establishing a Ministerial Covenant, the laying on of hands, prayer, and Communion. This service gives witness to God's continuing concern for the world by positioning a nation of priests after the order of Melchizedek Yeshua. It is here that GOD firmly places the calling and assignment upon their shoulders. These Ministers will be qualified to serve communion, conduct funerals, weddings, baptisms, and to lead the people of GOD as He establishes His Kingdom on earth. The ordination service expresses the supreme spirit of excellence and preparation to give glory to GOD, and to honor GOD's Divine appointment of an individual to the work of the Ministry.

THE ORDINATION SERVICE

Following the official notice of the CODA Ordination Committee's approval of the candidate for ordination, the Committee shall plan, **with the candidate,** for the Service of Ordination. The following list will serve as a guide for this important service:

A. Selection of persons to participate.

B. Send letters of invitation to all churches and guests.

C. Send an invitation and order of service to each participant invited.

D. Arrange for printed programs.

E. Have copies of the Operations & Procedure Manual.

F. Have instructions on proper attire.

H. Have the Certificate of Ordination properly filled out.

G. Arrange for special music in the service and a reception.

Order of Service:

- Song

- Scripture Reading

- Prayer

- Recommendation from the Ordination Committee

- Ordination Sermon

- Charge to the Candidate

- Charge to the Church

- Prayer

- Laying on of Hands

- Formal Signing of the Covenant and Code of Ethics

- Presentation of the Certificate

- Welcome into the Fellowship of Ministry

- Benediction

MINISTER'S LICENSE

'Likewise must the ministers be grave, not double-tongued, not given to much wine, not greedy of filthy lucre; Holding the mystery of the faith in a pure conscience. And let these also first be proved; then let them use the office of a (minister) deacon, being found blameless.'

1 Tim. 3:8-10

CODA Ministers Licensing and Ordination services are conducted annually on January 1st or June 7th. Prerequisites include the completion of a two year course of study, and successfully passing the licensing exam.* Licensing a Minister is distinct and different from Ordination. There are two levels of licenses. (1) The first level is the Ministerial License. As a Licensed Minister, you are qualified to conduct services, assist in serving communion, preach from the pulpit, teach RBS classes, and be the speaker for TMOT Radio Broadcast.

(2) The second is the License of Recognition. This license is designed to establish and prepare a student for the ministry. The License of Recognition also qualifies you to be called a minister. CODA Ministries has adapted the following order of service for licensing ministers:

- Prayer

- Scripture Reading

- Recommendation by the Pastor (and CMOC)

- Introduction of Moderator

- Licensing Sermon

- Charge to the Candidate/Prayer

- Presentation of the Pastor to the Candidates

- Presentation of the Certificate

- Benediction by Moderator

*Licenses may be presented to previously licensed ministers from another organization or church after becoming a member of CODA for a period of at least six (6) months, and having completed the licensing exam.

REMOVAL OR WITHDRAWAL OF ORDINATION

It is sometimes necessary to question the calling and ordination of a minister due to immoral or disorderly behavior or changes in his/her theological beliefs. Such questions may be directed to the Executive Board of CODA Ministries. Should they find there is substance to the charges, CODA Ministries Executive Board can withdraw or suspend recognition of ordination.

If a minister's recognition of ordination goes beyond the local church, and if just cause regarding immoral or unethical practices can be proven, CODA Ministries Executive Board may decide to withdraw or suspend recognition of ordination. Also, as it sometimes happens, a person may leave the active ordained Ministry for reasons other than retirement. Should the individual continue to lay claim to the privileges of a title in CODA, without being in Ministry, CODA Ministries Executive Board may withdraw their ordination.

Bibliography

Osborne, Grant R. "The Hermeneutical Spiral: (2010-02-25).

Henry A.Virkler "Hermeneutics Practical Rules for Biblical Interpretation." (2007)

Utley, R. J. D. (1996). 'You Can Understand the Bible' (p. 25).

J. Scott Duvall and J. Daniel Hays 'Grasping God's Word' (2004)

James Massey 'Designing the Sermon' Abingdon Preachers Library (1980)

Braga, James. 'How to Prepare Biblical Messages' Portland: Multnomah, (1981).

Christian Post "Recent Gallup Poll On American's View of Bible Reveals" ..

Christian History - 'Walk the Aisle' Christianity Today. (n.d.). (1944).

Leonard Ravenhill "Why Revival Tarries" Bethany House Publishers (2004)

Swanson, J., & Nave, O. 'New Nave's Topical Bible.' Oak Harbor (1994).

Blaise Pascal, page 75 of 'Pensees' New York; Penguin Books, (1966).

Elwell, W. A., & Beitzel, B. J. (1988). In Baker encyclopedia of the Bible

Bradshaw, Gordon E., Dr. (2010) "Prophetic Jumpstart"

Cook, Bruce, Dr. (2014-02-01). Partnering With The Prophetic: Portfolios, Protocols, Patterns & Processes

Dr. Glories Powell 'Yielding to the Power of the Prophetic' (2016)

Hamon, Bill; Roberts, Oral (2011-07-28). Prophets and Personal Prophecy: God's Prophetic Voice Today (p. 35). Destiny Image.

Watson, Thomas. 'The Mystery of the Lord's Supper' . Nashville: (2010-04-27)

'What is Baptism?' - Clarifying Christianity. (n.d.).

Bible Knowledge Commentary, John F. Walvoord and Roy B. Zuck, Victor Books (1983)

Eckman, J. P. (2002). Exploring church history (p. 98). Wheaton, IL: Crossway.

Frank Damazio "The Makings of a Leader" City Christian Publishing, (1988).

The New Ministers Manual, '<http://www.baylor.edu/content/services/document.php'>

Tom Chiarella   "How to Deliver a Eulogy" (2015)

"Building the Kingdom by Building People"